THE GENIUS KID'S GUIDE TO PRO BASEBALL

BY BRENDAN FLYNN

North Star KIDS

TABLE OF CONTENTS

THE HISTORY OF
MAJOR LEAGUE BASEBALL

The Boston Americans and the Pittsburgh Pirates faced off in the first World Series, which took place in 1903.

Major League Baseball (MLB) traces its roots back to the creation of the National League (NL) in 1876. Large cities in the United States had teams, including New York City; Chicago, Illinois; Philadelphia, Pennsylvania; and St. Louis, Missouri. Early stars such as New York Giants catcher Buck Ewing and Chicago Cubs first baseman Cap Anson attracted fans.

Baseball also has a painful history. For six decades, people running the sport stopped non-white players from joining the major leagues. Black ballplayers had to form their own teams and travel around the country seeking competition.

THE EARLY YEARS

The structure of professional baseball changed in its early years. The American Association served as the main rival to the NL from 1882 until it folded in 1891. The current MLB structure was born with the creation of the American League (AL) in 1900 and the rise of the World Series two years later.

Jackie Robinson, *left*, was the first Black player in the modern MLB era.

The early days of MLB are known as the dead-ball era. In those days, even the most powerful sluggers rarely hit more than ten home runs in a season. Philadelphia Athletics star John Franklin Baker led the AL in home runs for four straight seasons. However, he never hit more than 12 per season during that stretch.

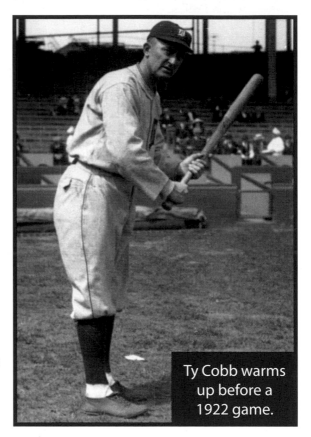

Ty Cobb warms up before a 1922 game.

The lack of home runs did not prevent the rise of incredible offensive talent. Detroit Tigers star Ty Cobb and his Pittsburgh Pirates counterpart Honus Wagner remain among the greatest hitters of all time. In addition, people flocked to watch legendary pitchers such as Washington Senators flamethrower Walter "Big Train" Johnson and New York Giants star Christy Mathewson. Many also went to see crafty pitcher Cy Young, who played for Cleveland in his early days. His major league record of 511 pitching victories is almost certain to remain unbroken.

In the 1920s, one man changed baseball forever. George Herman "Babe" Ruth brought in a new era with his many

Baseball legend Babe Ruth is at the center of the historic Red Sox–Yankees rivalry.

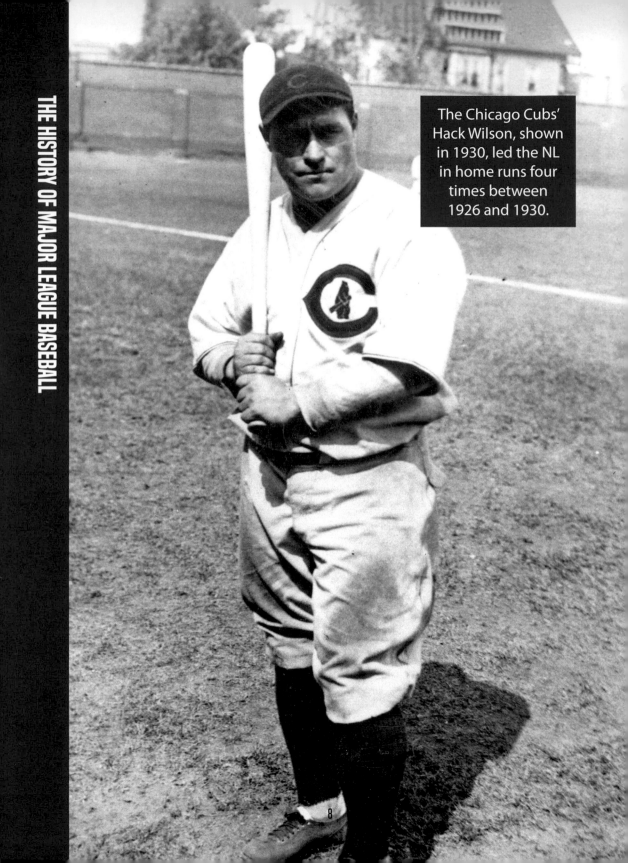

The Chicago Cubs' Hack Wilson, shown in 1930, led the NL in home runs four times between 1926 and 1930.

home runs. Fans came to ballparks to watch him smash pitches over the fence. Owners began to understand the lure of the home run. The dead-ball era was soon over, and the modern era of the game began.

Ruth teamed with iconic first baseman Lou Gehrig to help the New York Yankees create the first dynasty in baseball history. New York won six AL pennants and three World Series titles from 1921 to 1928. The 1927 club is still considered perhaps the greatest ever built.

The growing popularity of the sport in the 1920s was also driven by Hall of Famers such as St. Louis Cardinals slugger Rogers Hornsby, Chicago Cubs center fielder Hack Wilson, New York Giants right fielder Mel Ott, and Jimmie Foxx, who starred for both the Philadelphia Athletics and Boston Red Sox. Several pitchers also shone, including Athletics star Lefty Grove and right-hander Dizzy Dean, who led the Cardinals to a World Series crown in 1934. But the era was dominated by home run sluggers who sent fans hurrying to the ballparks.

THEY WERE ALL-STARS

Chicago mayor Edward J. Kelly wanted to create a sporting event for the 1933 World's Fair, which would take place in his city. *Chicago Tribune* sports editor Arch Ward came up with a plan. He organized the first All-Star Game. This was a battle between the best players from the AL and NL. A crowd of 47,595 people packed Comiskey Park. They watched a game that featured greats such as Babe Ruth and Jimmie Foxx. Ruth sparked a 4–2 AL victory with a home run. The All-Star Game has been an annual highlight of the baseball season ever since.

A NATIONAL PASTIME

MLB weathered many global crises, such as the Great Depression and World War II (1939–1945). It emerged in the late 1940s as the unquestioned national pastime. However, even during that time, Black players remained on the outside. Many of the premier baseball talents in the United States were forced to compete in separate organizations known as the Negro Leagues. There were no official rules against Black players joining major league clubs. But an unwritten agreement among owners prevented integration until 1946.

THE ONE-ARMED OUTFIELDER

Among the most amazing success stories in MLB history was that of Pete Gray. He played outfield for the Saint Louis Browns in 1945. Gray lost his right arm at age 12, when it was run over by a pickup truck. He played in 77 games and had a .218 batting average swinging with only his left arm. He would catch the baseball with a glove that he then placed on the stump under his right shoulder so he could throw the ball back.

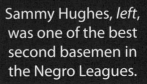

Sammy Hughes, *left*, was one of the best second basemen in the Negro Leagues.

That's when Brooklyn Dodgers owner Branch Rickey decided to shatter the racial barrier. He brought in a courageous and brilliant athlete named Jackie Robinson. The former college football and baseball star finally integrated the game for good on the first day of the 1947 season. Robinson thrived in Brooklyn. He won NL Rookie of the Year honors and forged a Hall of Fame career.

Soon other Black players were joining major league clubs. Cleveland outfielder Larry Doby became the first Black American Leaguer and also earned a spot in the Hall of Fame. Another was Giants star outfielder Monte Irvin, who appreciated what Robinson achieved for other Black players. "Jackie Robinson opened the door of baseball to all men," Irvin said after Robinson died in 1972. "He was the first to get the opportunity, but if he had not done such a great job, the path would have been so

Jackie Robinson did not take long to make an impact. He was the NL Rookie of the Year in 1947 and the NL MVP in 1949.

much more difficult. . . . Jack was the trailblazer and we are all deeply grateful."

Once the best athletes all got a chance to play, regardless of race, new superstars emerged. Those included the Giants' Willie Mays, whom many consider the greatest player of all time. Braves outfielder Hank Aaron began a successful attack on the all-time career home run record of 714 set by Ruth.

None of that changed a reality that proved annoying to fans outside of New York—the Yankees continued to dominate the sport. They won 15 of 18 AL pennants and ten World Series championships from 1947 to 1964. The Yankees continued to sign top-notch talent before the first amateur draft in 1965 evened out the playing field.

A number of great pitchers

Larry Doby, shown in 1951, played for Cleveland in the 1940s and 1950s.

Hank Aaron hits his 715th home run in 1974 to break Babe Ruth's record.

tilted the balance of the game in the 1960s. For the first time since before Ruth launched an offensive era nearly a half century earlier, teams began averaging four runs per game or fewer. Many fans found such low-scoring games boring. Attendance dropped considerably. MLB had to do something to attract fans who wanted to see more action. So it lowered the mound 5 inches (13 cm) in 1969 to make it tougher on pitchers. Four years later, the AL added a new position, the designated hitter. This player hit in place of the pitcher each time through the lineup. The moves worked. Soon more players were hitting the ball and more fans were coming to watch.

At the same time, baseball players were becoming a little

From the 1960s to the 1980s, Marvin Miller helped represent MLB players in disputes with team owners.

richer. They won a major battle against team owners in the 1970s. The league granted players free agency, or the right to sign with teams of their choosing once they spent a set number of years with their original teams. This increased the average salary of major league players.

However, some tension continued between players and team owners. This led to numerous strikes

THE CATCH

Cleveland set an AL record with 111 wins in 1954. They had stopped the Yankees dynasty for one season. And they were heavily favored to defeat the New York Giants in the World Series. In the eighth inning of Game 1 at the Polo Grounds in New York, the score was tied 2–2 when Cleveland's first two runners reached base. Up stepped Cleveland slugger Vic Wertz. He hit a booming drive to deep center field. It seemed impossible that even the speedy Willie Mays could reach the ball. But the Giants center fielder sprinted with his back to home plate and made an over-the-shoulder catch some 420 feet (128 m) from home plate. He then turned around while falling back. He fired the ball to the infield to keep the runners from scoring. Many consider it the greatest grab in baseball history. It has forever been known simply as "The Catch." The Giants won the game in extra innings and went on to sweep Cleveland in four games.

Some baseball fans protested the 1994 players' strike.

and lockouts that interrupted seasons. A two-month players' strike in 1981 led to the cancellation of 713 games. Another strike in 1994 ended the season in mid-August and wiped out the playoffs and World Series. Some fans resented the battles between the players and owners. They saw both sides as greedy.

EXPANSIONS, SETBACKS, AND DRAMA

Still, the league withstood that strife and kept growing. The AL and NL had just eight clubs each through 1960 and then ten through 1968. But expansion created new teams and appealed to fans in new markets from coast to coast. There have been 30 MLB teams since 1998. And whereas the regular-season winners in each league once met in the World Series, teams now must win at least three rounds of playoff games to snag a World Series crown.

In spite of this growth, baseball was having problems in the 1970s and 1980s. Among them was that football had surpassed it in overall popularity among US sports fans. They thought the pace of baseball was too slow. Baseball needed a jolt of energy, and it received one in the late 1990s.

WHAT'S ON TV?

Fans rarely watched baseball games involving teams outside their cities on television before the 1950s. That is when the *Game of the Week* was launched. One game was selected to be aired every Saturday during the baseball season until 1990, when the *Game of the Week* on NBC was canceled. CBS picked it up for three more years, but an increase in the number of games shown on cable ended the need for it.

MLB has a wild-card system. This allows two teams that didn't win their divisions to get into the playoffs. This system allowed the Washington Nationals to reach and win the World Series in 2019.

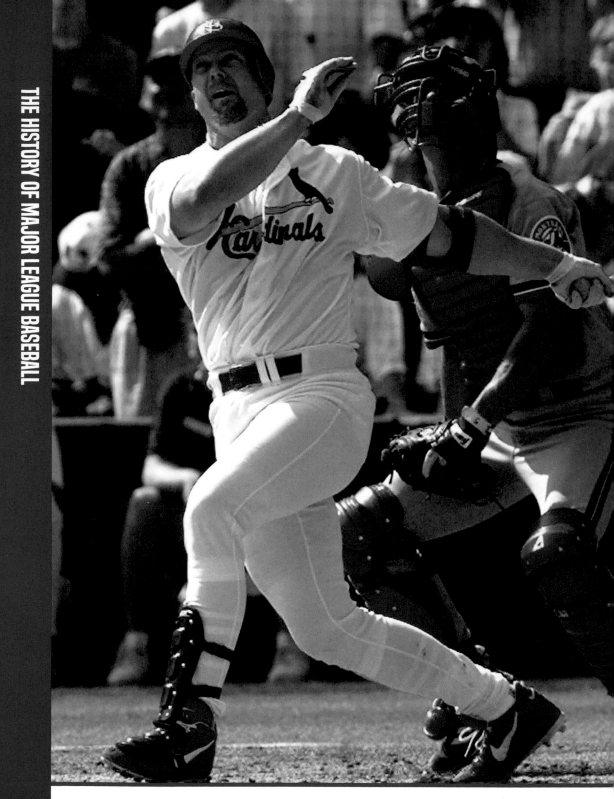

In 1998, Mark McGwire hit his 69th home run during a late September game.

In 1998, Cubs outfielder Sammy Sosa and Cardinals first baseman Mark McGwire provided drama. They staged an all-out assault on the home run mark of 61 in a single season, established by Yankees slugger Roger Maris in 1961. Sosa and McGwire began blasting baseballs at an incredible rate. Fans streamed back to ballparks. Both players had shattered the Maris mark by mid-September. The drama continued as the nation focused on which player would end the season with the new mark. McGwire earned that distinction when he smashed five home runs over the last weekend of the season to finish with 70 to Sosa's 66.

Meanwhile, San Francisco Giants superstar Barry Bonds followed the chase with interest and a bit of anger. The outfielder yearned for the national attention McGwire and Sosa had received.

Bonds bulked up further. Today, most people believe all three players used steroids to help achieve their power numbers. In any case, Bonds clobbered 73 home runs in 2001. He continued to smash home runs. In 2007, he overcame the career mark of 755 set by Hank Aaron in 1976.

But some fans believed the game had changed for the worse. They were bored with players swinging for the fences and the huge increase in home runs. They also yawned through games that featured strikeouts, which reached a rate of about one per half-inning. There were more strikeouts than hits for the first time in baseball history in 2018. Then it happened again in 2019. Games once lasted an average of two hours. Now, they were often taking more than three hours to

MLB's grueling 162-game season can be a grind for players, who often compete at least six days per week.

complete. There was too much time between pitches. Fans craved more action.

It seemed that baseball featured as many great athletes as ever. Hitters such as Los Angeles Angels outfielder Mike Trout, Los Angeles Dodgers first baseman Cody Bellinger, and Atlanta outfielder Ronald Acuña had an amazing mix of speed and power. Pitchers such as Washington Nationals ace Max Scherzer, Houston Astros star Justin Verlander, and Los Angeles Angels Shohei Ohtani continued to baffle opposing hitters. Pitchers were throwing harder than ever. Several could fire baseballs at more than 100 miles per hour (161 kmh).

But MLB had an identity problem. It was failing to successfully market its superstars. Some people said that the great Trout, a three-time AL most valuable player (MVP), could walk down the street of most US cities and not be recognized. Baseball once again faced a crossroads. The sport had been around since the 1860s thanks to its passionate fans. Many people believed the national pastime would soon find its way to another golden era.

AWARDING GREATNESS

A favorite topic of conversation during the baseball season is MLB's postseason awards and who's most likely to win them. The most prominent awards are those given to each league's most valuable player (MVP), top pitcher, and top rookie. Another annual award is the Gold Glove. This has been given by the baseball glove manufacturer Rawlings since 1957. It's awarded to the best fielder at each position. In 1980, the Silver Slugger Award was created. It was given to the top hitter at each position in each league.

Ronald Acuña
hits a home run
in a 2019 game.

Ketel Marte takes off after a hit during a 2021 game against the San Diego Padres.

TEAM HISTORY

Arizona has been hosting baseball teams for spring training since the 1940s. Many business leaders in Phoenix, Arizona, wanted the city to have its own major league team. However, MLB owners were worried about the summer temperatures in the desert city. When a plan emerged to build a retractable roof stadium in downtown Phoenix, the city was awarded an expansion team. The Diamondbacks began playing in the NL in 1998.

GREATEST PLAYERS

- **Jay Bell**, IF (1998–2002)
- **Steve Finley**, CF (1999–2004)
- **Paul Goldschmidt**, 1B (2011–18)
- **Luis Gonzalez**, LF (1999–2006)
- **Randy Johnson**, SP (1999–2004, 2007–08)
- **Ketel Marte**, 2B-OF (2017–)
- **A. J. Pollock**, CF (2012–18)
- **Curt Schilling**, SP (2000–03)
- **Justin Upton**, RF (2007–2012)
- **Brandon Webb**, SP (2003–2009)

In 2007, the Diamondbacks changed their colors from purple and teal to red and black.

TEAM STATS AND RECORDS*

ALL-TIME RECORD

- **Regular season:** 1,840–1,946
- **Postseason:** 18–22, one World Series title

TOP MANAGERS

- **Bob Melvin** (2005–09); 337–340 (regular season); 3–4 (postseason)
- **Kirk Gibson** (2010–14); 353–375 (regular season); 2–3 (postseason)

CAREER BATTING LEADERS

- **Home runs:** Luis Gonzalez, 224
- **RBIs:** Luis Gonzalez, 774
- **Runs:** Luis Gonzalez, 780
- **Hits:** Luis Gonzalez, 1,337
- **Games played:** Luis Gonzalez, 1,194

CAREER PITCHING LEADERS

- **Wins:** Randy Johnson, 118
- **Saves:** Jose Valverde, 98
- **Strikeouts:** Randy Johnson, 2,077
- **Shutouts:** Randy Johnson, 14

* All statistics in this book are through 2021

A PERFECT GAME

Randy Johnson was 40 years old when he threw the 17th perfect game in major league history. He retired all 27 batters he faced in a 2–0 victory at Atlanta on May 18, 2004. Johnson became the oldest pitcher in big-league history to throw a perfect game.

GREATEST SEASONS

In 2001, which was the Diamondbacks' fourth season, the team earned the NL West title. Then they won their first playoff series, besting the St. Louis Cardinals in the National League Division Series (NLDS) when Tony Womack singled home the winning run in the bottom of the ninth of the final game.

An easy win over the Atlanta Braves in the National League Championship Series (NLCS) set up a World Series showdown with the New York Yankees. It was a tense series. The Yankees got some late-game heroics to win Games 4 and 5 at Yankee Stadium.

The series shifted back to Phoenix, where the D-Backs evened the series with a blowout victory. Then, in a winner-take-all Game 7, the Yankees took a 2–1 lead into the bottom of the ninth. Their ace closer Mariano Rivera was on the mound. He had converted 23 straight save opportunities in the postseason. But the Diamondbacks rallied. Womack again had the big hit, a double that tied the game. Then Luis Gonzalez lifted a soft line drive just over the head of shortstop Derek Jeter to drive in the winning run as the Diamondbacks won their first World Series.

Luis Gonzalez reacts after driving in the winning run in the Diamondbacks' 3–2 victory in Game 7 of the 2001 World Series.

TEAM HISTORY

The Braves have called three cities home in their long history. The team traces its roots to Boston, Massachusetts, where it began playing as the Red Stockings in 1876, the first year of the NL. Over the years, they changed their nickname from Red Stockings to names such as Beaneaters, Doves, Rustlers, and Bees before finally settling on Braves in 1941.

The team generally played second fiddle to the more popular AL club, the Red Sox. So in 1953 the owners moved the Braves west to Milwaukee, Wisconsin. The Braves spent 13 years in Milwaukee before heading south to Atlanta, Georgia, where they have played since 1966.

Pitchers Warren Spahn, *left*, and Johnny Sain carried the Boston Braves to the 1948 World Series, but the Braves lost to Cleveland.

Between them, *from left*, Tom Glavine, John Smoltz, and Greg Maddux won six Cy Young Awards from 1991 to 1998 for the Braves.

GREATEST PLAYERS

- **Hank Aaron**, RF (1954–74)
- **Ronald Acuña**, OF (2018–)
- **Freddie Freeman**, 1B (2010–)
- **Tom Glavine**, LHP (1987–2002, 2008)
- **Chipper Jones**, 3B (1993, 1995–2012)
- **Greg Maddux**, RHP (1993–2003)
- **Eddie Mathews**, 3B (1952–66)
- **Dale Murphy**, OF (1976–90)
- **Kid Nichols**, RHP (1890–1901)
- **Phil Niekro**, RHP (1964–83, 1987)
- **John Smoltz**, RHP (1988–99, 2001–08)
- **Warren Spahn**, (1942, 1946–64)

TEAM STATS AND RECORDS

ALL-TIME RECORD
- **Regular season:** 10,820–10,757
- **Postseason:** 100–101, four World Series titles

TOP MANAGERS
- **Frank Selee** (1890–1901); 1,004–649 (regular season)
- **Bobby Cox** (1978–81, 1990–2010); 2,149–1,709 (regular season); 64–65, one World Series title (postseason)

CAREER BATTING LEADERS
- **Home runs:** Hank Aaron, 733
- **RBIs:** Hank Aaron, 2,202
- **Runs:** Hank Aaron, 2,107
- **Hits:** Hank Aaron, 3,600
- **Games played:** Hank Aaron, 3,076

CAREER PITCHING LEADERS
- **Wins:** Warren Spahn, 356
- **Saves:** Craig Kimbrel, 186
- **Strikeouts:** John Smoltz, 3,011
- **Shutouts:** Warren Spahn, 63

GREATEST SEASONS

The Braves have won the World Series four times. The first was in Boston in 1914. In 1957, the Braves faced the New York Yankees for the crown. Then in 1995, they beat Cleveland in six games.

BASEBALL BROTHERS

Hank and Tommie Aaron hold the MLB record for most combined home runs by two brothers with 768. Hank hit 755. Tommie hit 13.

In 2021, the Atlanta Braves took down the Houston Astros in six games. Outfielder Jorge Soler earned MVP honors after nailing three home runs in the series. The most memorable was a 446-foot (136 m) blast that broke a scoreless tie in Game 6. The monster home run cleared the seats and left the stadium.

Freddie Freeman earned the 2020 NL MVP Award.

TEAM HISTORY

Baltimore, Maryland, had hosted teams in the early days of both the NL and the AL. But the current Orioles trace their roots to the 1901 Milwaukee Brewers, who played just one year in the AL. They moved to St. Louis and changed their name to the Browns the next year. The Browns were usually among the worst teams in the AL. They had a hard time competing for fans with the crosstown rival Cardinals. So in 1954 the team moved to Baltimore and changed its name. The Orioles proved to be much more successful, winning four AL pennants and two World Series between 1966 and 1971. They also started the retro ballpark trend by opening Oriole Park at Camden Yards in 1992. And during the 1980s and 1990s, Cal Ripken Jr. made history as baseball's greatest iron man, playing 2,632 straight games.

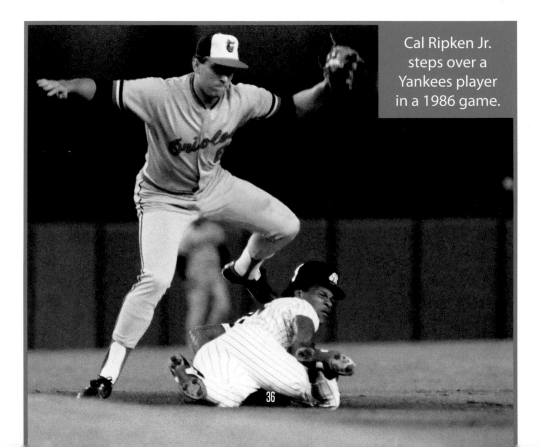

Cal Ripken Jr. steps over a Yankees player in a 1986 game.

GREATEST PLAYERS

- **Paul Blair**, CF (1964–76)
- **Manny Machado**, 3B (2012–18)
- **Eddie Murray**, 1B (1977–88, 1996)
- **Mike Mussina**, RHP (1991–2000)
- **Jim Palmer**, RHP (1965–67, 1969–84)
- **Boog Powell**, OF-1B (1961–74)
- **Cal Ripken Jr.**, SS-3B (1981–2001)
- **Brooks Robinson**, 3B (1955–77)
- **Frank Robinson**, OF (1966–71)
- **George Sisler**, 1B (1915–22, 1924–27)

Baltimore's Frank Robinson, *left*, and Brooks Robinson pose after the Orioles defeated the Dodgers in Game 1 of the 1966 World Series.

Cedric Mullins waits for a pitch during a 2021 game against the Tampa Bay Rays.

TEAM STATS AND RECORDS

ALL-TIME RECORD

- **Regular season:** 8,845–9,873
- **Postseason:** 54–44, three World Series titles

TOP MANAGERS

- **Earl Weaver** (1968–82, 1985–86); 1,480–1,060 (regular season); 26–20, one World Series title (postseason)
- **Buck Showalter** (2010–18); 669–684 (regular season); 6–8 (postseason)

CAREER BATTING LEADERS

- **Home runs:** Cal Ripken Jr., 431
- **RBIs:** Cal Ripken Jr., 1,695
- **Runs:** Cal Ripken Jr., 1,647
- **Hits:** Cal Ripken Jr., 3,184
- **Games played:** Cal Ripken Jr., 3,001

CAREER PITCHING LEADERS

- **Wins:** Jim Palmer, 268
- **Saves:** Gregg Olson, 160
- **Strikeouts:** Jim Palmer, 2,212
- **Shutouts:** Jim Palmer, 53

GREATEST SEASONS

By 1966, the Orioles had been in Baltimore for more than a decade without winning a pennant. But they'd been getting young talent, especially on the mound. In 1966, their aces were 23-year-old lefty Dave McNally and 20-year-old right-hander Jim Palmer. Veteran outfielder Frank Robinson won the AL MVP Award after getting 49 home runs and 122 runs batted in (RBIs). Third baseman Brooks Robinson anchored the infield. The Orioles won the league by nine games. But they were World Series underdogs against the playoff-tested Los Angeles Dodgers, who had won the title in 1963 and 1965. Still, the NL champs proved to be no match for Baltimore's pitching. The Dodgers were held scoreless for the final 33 innings in a four-game sweep, giving the Orioles their first title.

WINNING PITCHERS

One of the things that made the Orioles consistent winners in the Earl Weaver era was their pitching. From 1968 through 1980, they had at least one pitcher who won 20 games every year. In 1971, they became just the second team in major league history to have four 20-game winners in one season. They were Mike Cuellar (20–9), Pat Dobson (20–8), Dave McNally (21–5), and Jim Palmer (20–9).

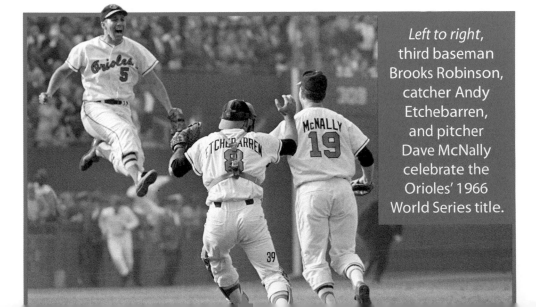

Left to right, third baseman Brooks Robinson, catcher Andy Etchebarren, and pitcher Dave McNally celebrate the Orioles' 1966 World Series title.

BOSTON RED SOX

TEAM HISTORY

Boston was home to one of the teams that founded the AL in 1901. First known as the Americans, they changed their name to the Red Sox in 1908. They were one of the dominant teams in MLB's early days, winning five World Series by 1918. However, in 1920 their cash-strapped owner sold promising young slugger Babe Ruth to the New York Yankees. The so-called Curse of the Bambino was born. The Yankees raced past their rivals to become kings of the AL for the rest of the century. Meanwhile, the Red Sox went more than 80 years before winning their next title. Still, thanks to historic Fenway Park and some of the greatest players ever to set foot on a diamond, the Red Sox have long been one of the league's most recognizable teams.

Hall of Famer Wade Boggs won four consecutive batting titles from 1985 to 1988.

Rafael Devers slides home in a 2021 game.

GREATEST PLAYERS

- **Wade Boggs**, 3B (1982–92)
- **Roger Clemens**, RHP (1984–96)
- **Dwight Evans**, RF (1972–91)
- **Carlton Fisk**, C (1969, 1971–80)
- **Pedro Martínez**, RHP (1998–2004)
- **David Ortiz**, DH (2003–16)
- **Dustin Pedroia**, 2B (2007–19)
- **Ted Williams**, OF (1939–42, 1946–60)
- **Carl Yastrzemski**, OF (1961–83)
- **Cy Young**, SP (1901–08)

TEAM STATS AND RECORDS

ALL-TIME RECORD

- **Regular season:** 9,718–9,014
- **Postseason:** 108–91, nine World Series titles

TOP MANAGERS

- **Joe Cronin** (1935–47); 1,071–916 (regular season); 3–4 (postseason)
- **Terry Francona** (2004–11); 744–552 (regular season); 28–17, two World Series titles (postseason)

CAREER BATTING LEADERS

- **Home runs:** Ted Williams, 521
- **RBIs:** Carl Yastrzemski, 1,844
- **Runs:** Carl Yastrzemski, 1,816
- **Hits:** Carl Yastrzemski, 3,419
- **Games played:** Carl Yastrzemski, 3,308

Fans hoped Carl Yastrzemski, *left*, and Tony Conigliaro could bring the Red Sox another World Series title in the 1960s.

CAREER PITCHING LEADERS

- **Wins:** Roger Clemens, Cy Young, 192
- **Saves:** Jonathan Papelbon, 219
- **Strikeouts:** Roger Clemens, 2,590
- **Shutouts:** Roger Clemens, Cy Young, 38

GREATEST SEASONS

To say the Red Sox entered the 2004 season in a drought would be an understatement. They had last won the World Series in 1918. The previous year they'd lost the American League Championship Series (ALCS) to their hated rivals, the Yankees, on a walk-off home run in extra innings of Game 7. But Boston fans would not have to endure much more heartbreak. The 2004 ALCS was a rematch of the previous season. This time the Yankees won the first three games. No team had ever come back from that. But Boston rallied to win Game 4 in extra innings. They did the same thing in Game 5. Then they won two straight at Yankee Stadium to slay that dragon. Sweeping the St. Louis Cardinals in the World Series felt almost like an afterthought, but it clinched Boston's first world championship in 86 years.

DUSTIN PEDROIA

Dustin Pedroia was named the 2007 AL Rookie of the Year after hitting .317 and driving in 50 runs while helping Boston win the AL East and World Series. One year later, Pedroia was the AL's MVP. The second baseman hit .326 with 83 RBIs and 20 stolen bases. He also won a Gold Glove Award that season.

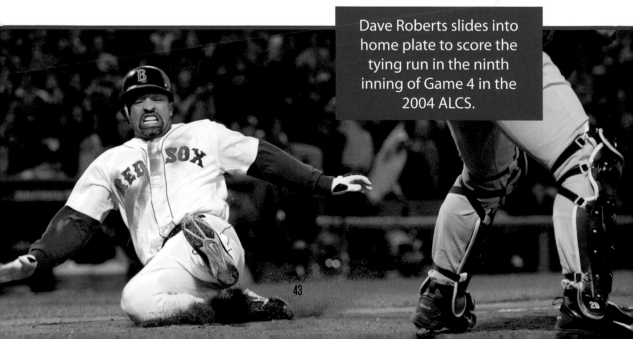

Dave Roberts slides into home plate to score the tying run in the ninth inning of Game 4 in the 2004 ALCS.

TEAM HISTORY

The Chicago White Stockings were one of the founding members of the NL in 1876. Despite the similarity in names, this is not the team that became the AL's White Sox. Instead, the NL squad became the Colts in 1890 and the Orphans in 1898. They finally settled on Cubs in 1903. They've played their home games at the ivy-walled Wrigley Field since 1914. Once one of the most powerful clubs in the league, the Cubs went from 1909 to 2015 without winning the World Series. Regardless, they kept a massive fan base.

Ernie Banks was the NL MVP twice during his 19 seasons in Chicago. He was enshrined in the Hall of Fame in 1977.

Kyle Hendricks pitches during an August 2021 game.

GREATEST PLAYERS

- **Cap Anson**, 1B-Mgr (1876–97)
- **Ernie Banks**, SS-1B (1953–71)
- **Gabby Hartnett**, C (1922–41)
- **Anthony Rizzo**, 1B (2012–21)
- **Ryne Sandberg**, 2B (1982–94, 1996–97)
- **Ron Santo**, 3B (1960–73)
- **Lee Smith**, RHP (1980–87)
- **Sammy Sosa**, RF (1992–2004)
- **Billy Williams**, OF-1B (1959–74)
- **Hack Wilson**, OF (1926–31)

TEAM STATS AND RECORDS

ALL-TIME RECORD

- **Regular season**: 11,087–10,521
- **Postseason**: 47–75, three World Series titles

TOP MANAGERS

- **Cap Anson** (1879–97); 1,282–932 (regular season)
- **Charlie Grimm** (1932–38, 1944–49, 1960); 946–782 (regular season); 5–12 (postseason)

CAREER BATTING LEADERS

- **Home runs**: Sammy Sosa, 545
- **RBIs**: Cap Anson, 1,880
- **Runs**: Cap Anson, 1,722
- **Hits**: Cap Anson, 3,012
- **Games played**: Ernie Banks, 2,528

CAREER PITCHING LEADERS

- **Wins**: Charlie Root, 201
- **Saves**: Lee Smith, 180
- **Strikeouts**: Fergie Jenkins, 2,038
- **Shutouts**: Mordecai Brown, 48

Sammy Sosa swings during a 1998 game at Wrigley Field.

GREATEST SEASONS

The Cubs had a handful of painful defeats in the pursuit of their third World Series title. In 2003, for example, they were just five outs away from defeating the Florida Marlins in the NLCS before suffering an epic collapse. Fans might've expected more of the same in 2016. Instead, the Cubs reached the World Series. When Chicago lost three of the first four games against Cleveland, it appeared the Cubs were headed for another heartbreak. But the bats got hot and the pitching was just good enough for them to win the final three games. In the tenth inning of Game 7, third baseman Kris Bryant sealed the Cubs' title when he fielded a ground ball and threw across the diamond to Anthony Rizzo for the third out. Cubs fans finally had the victory they'd been waiting for.

The Cubs celebrate their 2016 World Series victory.

THE CURSE OF THE BILLY GOAT

On October 6, 1945, the Cubs hosted the Detroit Tigers at Wrigley Field in Game 4 of the World Series. William "Billy Goat" Sianis bought two tickets for the game: one for him and one for his goat Murphy. However, Sianis and Murphy were ordered to leave because the goat smelled bad. When Sianis was leaving, he reportedly said that the Cubs "ain't gonna win no more." The Cubs did not return to the World Series until 2016.

José Abreu swings for a home run in a 2021 game against the St. Louis Cardinals.

TEAM HISTORY

Dating back to 1901, the White Sox are a franchise rich with history and controversy. Key members of the 1919 "Black Sox" admitted to losing the World Series on purpose after taking bribes from gamblers. Eight players were banned from baseball. Some believe that incident might have triggered some type of curse for the team. The White Sox didn't win another AL pennant for 40 years, and they lost to the Los Angeles Dodgers in the 1959 World Series. They would go on to win just three division titles over the next 45 years, failing to advance in the playoffs each time. Finally, in 2005, the White Sox delivered a World Series title to their loyal fans on Chicago's South Side.

GREATEST PLAYERS

- **José Abreu**, 1B-DH (2014–)
- **Luke Appling**, SS (1930–43, 1945–50)
- **Mark Buehrle**, LHP (2000–11)
- **Eddie Collins**, 2B (1915–26)
- **Carlton Fisk**, C (1981–93)
- **Joe Jackson**, OF (1915–20)
- **Paul Konerko**, 1B (1999–14)
- **Ted Lyons**, RHP (1923–42, 1946)
- **Billy Pierce**, LHP (1949–61)
- **Frank Thomas**, 1B-DH (1990–2005)

A WHITE SOX PERFECT GAME

Mark Buehrle made history on July 23, 2009, against the Tampa Bay Rays. He took a perfect game into the ninth. Dewayne Wise, just inserted into center field, made a leaping catch above the fence to steal a potential leadoff homer in the ninth from Gabe Kapler. Buehrle then retired the final two hitters to nail the second perfect game in White Sox history.

Frank Thomas was one of baseball's best hitters during the 1990s.

TEAM STATS AND RECORDS

ALL-TIME RECORD

- **Regular season:** 9,411–9,309
- **Postseason:** 30–32, three World Series titles

TOP MANAGERS

- **Jimmy Dykes** (1934–46); 899–940 (regular season)
- **Al López** (1957–65, 1968–69); 840–650 (regular season); 2–4 (postseason)

CAREER BATTING LEADERS

- **Home runs:** Frank Thomas, 448
- **RBIs:** Frank Thomas, 1,465
- **Runs:** Frank Thomas, 1,327
- **Hits:** Luke Appling, 2,749
- **Games played:** Luke Appling, 2,422

CAREER PITCHING LEADERS

- **Wins:** Ted Lyons, 260
- **Saves:** Bobby Thigpen, 201
- **Strikeouts:** Billy Pierce, 1,796
- **Shutouts:** Ed Walsh, 57

GREATEST SEASONS

A dominant pitching staff led the 2005 White Sox to 99 victories. That was the most in the AL that season. Four Chicago starters won at least 14 games. Closer Dustin Hermanson posted 34 of the team's 54 saves, and the White Sox led the AL with a 3.61 earned-run average (ERA). And that was just in the regular season. In the postseason, Chicago's pitchers got a 2.55 ERA as they mowed down opponent after opponent. The White Sox lost just one game in three series. Then they swept the Houston Astros in the World Series. The win put an end to talk of a Black Sox curse once and for all.

Catcher A. J. Pierzynski jumps into closer Bobby Jenks's arms as third baseman Joe Crede joins the celebration on October 26, 2005. The White Sox had just defeated the Astros 1–0 to earn a World Series sweep.

CINCINNATI REDS

TEAM HISTORY

In 1882, the Cincinnati Red Stockings joined the American Association, which was considered a major league at the time. Eight years later, they dropped the "Stockings" and moved to the NL. The Cincinnati Reds have been part of the NL ever since. Some of the greatest players in MLB history have played for the Reds. Many of them were part of the "Big Red Machine," which won six division titles and two World Series in the 1970s.

GREATEST PLAYERS

- **Johnny Bench**, C (1967–83)
- **Dave Concepción**, SS (1970–88)
- **Barry Larkin**, SS (1986–2004)
- **Joe Morgan**, 2B (1972–79)
- **Tony Pérez**, 1B (1964–76, 1984–86)
- **Vada Pinson**, CF (1958–68)
- **Frank Robinson**, OF (1956–65)
- **Pete Rose**, OF-3B (1963–78, 1984–86)
- **Edd Roush**, CF (1917–26, 1931)
- **Joey Votto**, 1B (2007–)

Pete Rose was one of the top hitters in baseball history. He led the NL in hits seven times and finished his career as baseball's all-time hits leader.

Joey Votto was the 2010 NL MVP.

TEAM STATS AND RECORDS

ALL-TIME RECORD
- **Regular season**: 10,713–10,501
- **Postseason**: 49–48, five World Series titles

TOP MANAGERS
- **Bill McKechnie** (1938–46); 744–631 (regular season); 4–7, one World Series title (postseason)
- **Sparky Anderson** (1970–78); 863–586 (regular season); 26–16, two World Series titles (postseason)

CAREER BATTING LEADERS
- **Home runs**: Johnny Bench, 389
- **RBIs**: Johnny Bench, 1,376
- **Runs**: Pete Rose, 1,741
- **Hits**: Pete Rose, 3,358
- **Games played**: Pete Rose, 2,722

CAREER PITCHING LEADERS
- **Wins**: Eppa Rixey, 179
- **Saves**: Danny Graves, 182
- **Strikeouts**: Jim Maloney, 1,592
- **Shutouts**: Bucky Walters, 32

BAD TEAM, BIG MOMENTS

The 1934 and 1935 Reds were downright awful, averaging just 60 wins per season. But they did boast two distinctions. They became the first MLB team to travel by airplane when they flew from Cincinnati to Chicago on June 8, 1934. They also hosted the first night game in MLB history. Cincinnati beat the Phillies under the lights on May 24, 1935, in front of 20,422 fans at Crosley Field.

GREATEST SEASONS

Led by 36-year-old rookie manager Sparky Anderson, the 1970 Reds won 102 games and reached the World Series, losing to the Baltimore Orioles in five games. Two years later they were back. But they lost again, this time to the Oakland Athletics in seven games. Those defeats set the stage for one of the most dominant

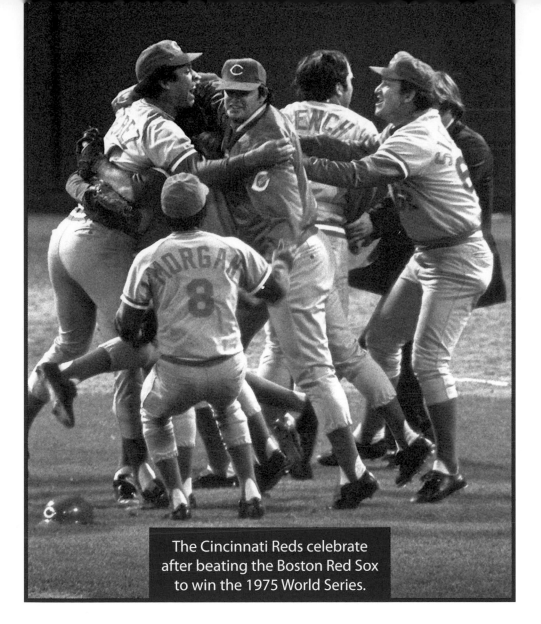

The Cincinnati Reds celebrate after beating the Boston Red Sox to win the 1975 World Series.

two-season runs in MLB history. The 1975 Reds won 108 games in the regular season, winning the NL West by a whopping 20 games. They faced the Boston Red Sox in an epic World Series. Cincinnati clinched it with a 4–3 victory in Game 7 at Boston's Fenway Park. The core of the "Big Red Machine" was back in 1976 when the Reds won 102 games. They swept the Philadelphia Phillies in the NLCS. Then they wiped out the New York Yankees in four straight games to win their second consecutive World Series.

Emmanuel Clase delivers a pitch during a June 2021 game.

TEAM HISTORY

Cleveland, Ohio, has been home to an AL baseball team since 1901. The team itself has had many nicknames over the years. Starting in 1915 they were called the Indians. But as time went on, the team wanted a new nickname that wasn't insensitive to Native Americans. In 2021, the team was renamed the Cleveland Guardians.

Historically, the team has had two strong eras that bookend a long stretch of losses. In the 1940s and 1950s, Cleveland was one of the few teams to challenge the New York Yankees for supremacy in the AL. In fact, the Yankees won every AL pennant from 1947 to 1958 except the ones that Cleveland claimed in 1948 and 1954. Then after some mighty lean years, the club had a resurgence in the mid-1990s after opening a new ballpark in 1994.

GREATEST PLAYERS

- **Earl Averill**, OF (1929–39)
- **Lou Boudreau**, SS (1938–50)
- **Stan Coveleski**, RHP (1916–24)
- **Larry Doby**, OF (1947–55, 1958)
- **Bob Feller**, RHP (1936–41, 1945–56)
- **Nap Lajoie**, 1B-2B (1902–14)
- **Bob Lemon**, RHP (1941–42, 1946–58)
- **Kenny Lofton**, OF (1992–96, 1998–2001, 2007)
- **Tris Speaker**, OF (1916–26)
- **Jim Thome**, 3B-1B-DH (1991–2002, 2011)

FRANK ROBINSON

Cleveland made history when it hired Frank Robinson in October 1974 as the first Black manager in MLB history. Robinson served as both a player and manager with Cleveland at first. He gave fans something to remember by smashing a home run in his first at bat on Opening Day in 1975. His teams went 186–189 during his two and a half seasons in charge. The Hall of Famer spent 16 years as a manager with four franchises.

TEAM STATS AND RECORDS

ALL-TIME RECORD

- **Regular season:** 9,592–9,144
- **Postseason:** 56–55, two World Series titles

TOP MANAGERS

- **Lou Boudreau** (1942–50); 728–649 (regular season); 4–2, one World Series title (postseason)
- **Mike Hargrove** (1991–99); 721–591 (regular season); 27–25 (postseason)

CAREER BATTING LEADERS

- **Home runs:** Jim Thome, 337
- **RBIs:** Earl Averill, 1,084
- **Runs:** Earl Averill, 1,154
- **Hits:** Nap Lajoie, 2,047
- **Games played:** Terry Turner, 1,619

CAREER PITCHING LEADERS

- **Wins:** Bob Feller, 266
- **Saves:** Cody Allen, 149
- **Strikeouts:** Bob Feller, 2,581
- **Shutouts:** Addie Joss, 45

Hall of Fame right-hander Bob Feller was a key to Cleveland's success in the 1940s and 1950s.

GREATEST SEASONS

Jacobs Field, a ballpark built in downtown Cleveland, opened in 1994. Its sole tenant hadn't made the postseason in 40 years, but the ballpark provided a much-needed jolt of energy to the franchise. Beginning in 1995, Cleveland won five straight AL Central titles. Jacobs Field hosted World Series games against the Atlanta Braves in 1995 and the Florida Marlins in 1997, though the home club suffered heartbreaking defeats both years. The club returned to the World Series in 2016, this time facing the Chicago Cubs, the only team as star-crossed as their own. Cleveland's hopes again were dashed when the Cubs rallied to win Games 6 and 7 on the road. But hopes remain high that happy days will return to the ballpark, now known as Progressive Field.

Jacobs Field is shown in April 1994 during the first regular-season game at the ballpark. Cleveland began a successful period that year.

COLORADO ROCKIES

Charlie Blackmon watches his home run during a 2021 game against the San Diego Padres.

TEAM HISTORY

In the early 1990s, the NL was looking to expand. Denver, Colorado, had long been a successful minor league city. A few MLB teams had considered moving there over the years. Finally, the league awarded Denver an expansion team. The Colorado Rockies played their first season in 1993. Baseballs soon began flying out of their home park. The high altitude in the mountains creates dry air that takes the moisture out of baseballs. That causes the balls to travel farther than at lower elevations. MLB tried a number of methods to slow down the home run pace in Denver. One that seemed to work best was storing the game balls in a humidor to maintain their moisture. But the ball still seems to jump off players' bats in the Mile High City.

GREATEST PLAYERS

- **Nolan Arenado**, 3B (2013–20)
- **Charlie Blackmon**, OF (2011–)
- **Vinny Castilla**, 3B (1993–99, 2004, 2006)
- **Aaron Cook**, RHP (2002–11)
- **Carlos Gonzalez**, OF (2009–18)
- **Todd Helton**, 1B (1997–2013)
- **Matt Holliday**, LF (2004–08, 2018)
- **Ubaldo Jiménez**, RHP (2006–11)
- **Trevor Story**, SS (2016–)
- **Troy Tulowitzki**, SS (2006–15)

Ubaldo Jiménez fires a pitch in 2009. Jiménez had a breakout year with 15 wins and helped Colorado make the playoffs. In 2010, he pitched even better, finishing 19–8 with a 2.88 ERA.

TEAM STATS AND RECORDS

ALL-TIME RECORD

- **Regular season:** 2,133–2,401
- **Postseason:** 10–14

TOP MANAGERS

- **Don Baylor** (1993–98); 440–469 (regular season); 1–3 (postseason)
- **Clint Hurdle** (2002–09); 534–625 (regular season); 7–4 (postseason)

CAREER BATTING LEADERS

- **Home runs:** Todd Helton, 369
- **RBIs:** Todd Helton, 1,406
- **Runs:** Todd Helton, 1,401
- **Hits:** Todd Helton, 2,519
- **Games played:** Todd Helton, 2,247

CAREER PITCHING LEADERS

- **Wins:** Jorge De La Rosa, 86
- **Saves:** Brian Fuentes, 115
- **Strikeouts:** Jorge De La Rosa, 985
- **Shutouts:** Jason Jennings and Ubaldo Jiménez, 3

COORS FIELD

At Coors Field, almost all of the seats are green. One row, however, is colored purple. That row is marked because it is exactly 1 mile (1.6 km) above sea level.

GREATEST SEASONS

The Rockies made the playoffs just once in their first 14 seasons. And their prospects for 2007 looked bleak in mid-September when they were stuck in fourth place in the NL West. Then the team got white-hot. The Rockies won 13 of their last 14 games, including a 4–3 victory over the first-place Arizona Diamondbacks on the final day of the season. That tied them with the San Diego Padres for second place in the West and forced a one-game playoff to

A banged-up Matt Holliday lies on the ground after scoring the winning run for the 2007 NL wild-card spot.

determine the NL wild-card winner. San Diego scored twice in the top of the 13th to take an 8–6 lead. But the Rockies' magic continued. Matt Holliday's triple tied the game. Then he scored on a sacrifice fly to give Colorado the victory.

But the Rockies weren't done. They swept the Phillies and D-Backs in their next two series to earn their first World Series appearance. That made it an incredible 21 wins in 22 games. The Boston Red Sox ended that run with a four-game sweep. But the Rockies had given their fans a playoff run to remember.

DETROIT TIGERS

TEAM HISTORY

The Detroit Tigers date back to the founding of the AL in 1901. Led by the great Ty Cobb, they won three straight AL pennants from 1907 to 1909 but couldn't bring home a World Series title. They had another surge with four AL championships between 1934 and 1945. This time they won a World Series in 1935. Then they won another ten years later. Two more titles came in 1968 and 1984. Some tough years were not far away, though. Starting in 2001, the Tigers had one of the worst stretches in team history, losing 96, 106, and 119 games over the next three seasons. They rebounded to reach the World Series in 2006 and made four straight playoff appearances starting in 2011.

GREATEST PLAYERS

- **Miguel Cabrera**, 3B-1B-DH (2008–)
- **Norm Cash**, 1B (1960–74)
- **Ty Cobb**, OF (1905–26)
- **Charlie Gehringer**, 2B (1924–42)
- **Hank Greenberg**, 1B-OF (1930, 1933–41, 1945–46)
- **Harry Heilmann**, OF-IF (1914, 1916–29)
- **Al Kaline**, OF (1953–74)
- **Alan Trammell**, SS (1977–96)
- **Justin Verlander**, SP (2005–17)
- **Lou Whitaker**, 2B (1977–95)

AVOIDING THE BOTTOM

The New York Mets finished an MLB-worst 40–120 in their first season in 1962. No other MLB team has lost that many games in a season. But the Tigers came close in 2003. They had 118 losses with six games still to play. The Tigers were on the verge of tying or breaking the record. Instead, they won five out of their last six games to avoid being a bad part of baseball history.

Tigers designated hitter Carlos Guillen congratulates first baseman Miguel Cabrera after Cabrera scored during a 2010 game. Cabrera led the AL in RBIs that season.

TEAM STATS AND RECORDS

ALL-TIME RECORD

- **Regular season**: 9,446–9,311
- **Postseason**: 57–62, four World Series titles

TOP MANAGERS

- **Hughie Jennings** (1907–20); 1,131–972 (regular season); 4–12 (postseason)
- **Sparky Anderson** (1979–95); 1,331–1,248 (regular season); 8–5, one World Series title (postseason)

CAREER BATTING LEADERS

- **Home runs**: Al Kaline, 399
- **RBIs**: Ty Cobb, 1,811
- **Runs**: Ty Cobb, 2,087
- **Hits**: Ty Cobb, 3,900
- **Games played**: Al Kaline, 2,834

CAREER PITCHING LEADERS

- **Wins**: Hooks Dauss, 223
- **Saves**: Todd Jones, 235
- **Strikeouts**: Mickey Lolich, 2,679
- **Shutouts**: Mickey Lolich, 39

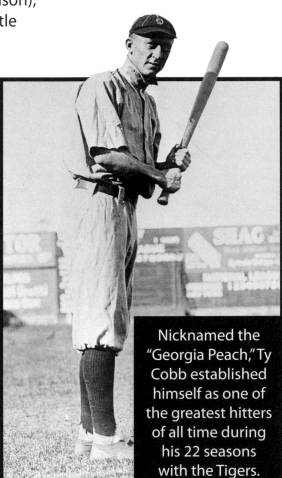

Nicknamed the "Georgia Peach," Ty Cobb established himself as one of the greatest hitters of all time during his 22 seasons with the Tigers.

Alan Trammell, *left*, Willie Hernandez, *center*, and Darrell Evans celebrate after the Tigers beat the Kansas City Royals in the 1984 ALCS.

GREATEST SEASONS

The 1984 Tigers were dominant. They started the season with an MLB-record 35 wins in their first 40 games. And they kept it up thanks to a team of talented players. Second baseman Lou Whitaker, catcher Lance Parrish, and center fielder Chet Lemon were in the AL starting lineup at the All-Star Game—with shortstop Alan Trammell and pitchers Jack Morris and Willie Hernandez named reserves. Parrish, Trammell, and Whitaker all won AL Gold Gloves. Parrish and Whitaker also added AL Silver Slugger Awards as the best batters at their positions. The Tigers finished the season 104–58. They swept the Kansas City Royals in the ALCS. Then they defeated the San Diego Padres in five games to win the World Series.

HOUSTON ASTROS

TEAM HISTORY

The Astros began playing in the NL in 1962. They were known as the Houston Colt .45s. Three years later, they changed their name to Astros. This was a nod to Texas's status as the hub of the US aerospace industry. That year was also notable for another historic event: the opening of the Astrodome. It was MLB's first domed stadium.

The Astros spent their first 51 seasons in the NL. They often reached the playoffs, but they won just one pennant. In 2013, they agreed to move to the

Second baseman Craig Biggio, *left*, and first baseman Jeff Bagwell played together for Houston from 1991 to 2005.

The Astrodome is shown in the 1980s. The domed stadium was the Astros' home from 1965 to 1999.

AL West in order to balance the number of teams in each league. That year, the Astros lost 111 games. However, they were amassing young talent that enabled a quick turnaround, leading to the team's first World Series title in 2017.

GREATEST PLAYERS

- **José Altuve**, 2B (2011–)
- **Jeff Bagwell**, 1B (1991–2005)
- **Lance Berkman**, OF-1B (1999–2010)
- **Craig Biggio**, C-2B-OF (1988–2007)
- **César Cedeño**, CF (1970–81)
- **Carlos Correa**, SS (2015–)
- **José Cruz**, LF (1975–87)
- **Larry Dierker**, RHP (1964–76)
- **Roy Oswalt**, RHP (2001–10)
- **Jimmy Wynn**, OF (1963–73)

TEAM STATS AND RECORDS

ALL-TIME RECORD

- **Regular season**: 4,725–4,764
- **Postseason**: 66–69, one World Series title

TOP MANAGERS

- **Bill Virdon** (1975–82); 544–522 (regular season); 4–6 (postseason)
- **A. J. Hinch** (2015–19); 481–329 (regular season); 28–22, one World Series title (postseason)

CAREER BATTING LEADERS

- **Home runs**: Jeff Bagwell, 449
- **RBIs**: Jeff Bagwell, 1,529
- **Runs**: Craig Biggio, 1,844
- **Hits**: Craig Biggio, 3,060
- **Games played**: Craig Biggio, 2,850

CAREER PITCHING LEADERS

- **Wins**: Joe Niekro, 144
- **Saves**: Billy Wagner, 225
- **Strikeouts**: Nolan Ryan, 1,866
- **Shutouts**: Larry Dierker, 25

BIGGIO AND BAGWELL

Craig Biggio appeared in 50 games in 1988. He quickly became a regular in the Houston lineup, playing catcher, outfield, and second baseman during his career. In 1991, Jeff Bagwell made his debut as a first baseman for the Astros. Together, Biggio and Bagwell led the Astros for the next 15 years. Both players spent their entire careers with Houston. Their names dominate the Astros' record book.

GREATEST SEASONS

The Astros cruised to 101 wins and a division title in 2017, thanks in large part to their smallest player. Second baseman José Altuve—generously listed at 5-foot-6—led the majors with a .346 batting average. He also hit 24 home runs, stole 32 bases, and won the AL MVP Award. Altuve had plenty of help, of course. Center fielder George Springer blasted 34 homers, shortstop Carlos Correa hit .315 with 24 home runs, and utility man Marwin González hit .303 with a team-high 90 RBIs. Houston knocked out two AL East titans—the Red Sox and the Yankees—in the AL playoffs. Then in a wild World Series, the Astros won Game 7 in Los Angeles to beat the Dodgers for their first world championship.

Astros players pour onto the field to celebrate their 2017 World Series victory.

71

TEAM HISTORY

Kansas City, Missouri, was a minor league town until the Philadelphia Athletics moved there in 1955. But the Athletics didn't stick around long. They moved to the West Coast after 13 straight losing seasons. Still, Kansas City wasn't done as a major league market. The Royals came to town in 1969.

The Kansas City Royals posted a winning season in their third year. They were challenging for the division title by their seventh. Then from 1976 to 1980, they won four division titles. They finally reached the World Series in 1980, but they lost to the Philadelphia Phillies in six games. Five years later, the Royals won their first title. They got their second title in 2015. The team's journey has proven that Kansas City is indeed a major league town.

Salvador Pérez races to first base in a 2021 game against the Red Sox.

GREATEST PLAYERS

- **Kevin Appier**, RHP (1989–99, 2003–04)
- **George Brett**, 3B (1973–93)
- **Alex Gordon**, LF (2007–20)
- **Mark Gubicza**, RHP (1984–96)
- **Hal McRae**, DH-OF (1973–87)
- **Amos Otis**, CF (1970–83)
- **Salvador Pérez**, C (2011–18, 2020–)
- **Bret Saberhagen**, RHP (1984–91)
- **Frank White**, 2B (1973–90)
- **Willie Wilson**, OF (1976–90)

TWO MISSOURI TEAMS

Kansas City and St. Louis are located 249 miles (400 km) apart along Interstate 70 in Missouri. The 1985 World Series was thus known as the I-70 Series. It featured the Kansas City Royals and the St. Louis Cardinals. After the Royals won, third baseman George Brett said of the Cardinals, "We showed 'em."

TEAM STATS AND RECORDS

ALL-TIME RECORD

- **Regular season:** 4,001–4,344
- **Postseason:** 40–34, two World Series titles

TOP MANAGERS

- **Whitey Herzog** (1975–79); 410–304 (regular season); 5–9 (postseason)
- **Ned Yost** (2010–19); 457–502 (regular season); 22–9, one World Series title (postseason)

CAREER BATTING LEADERS

- **Home runs:** George Brett, 317
- **RBIs:** George Brett, 1,596
- **Runs:** George Brett, 1,583
- **Hits:** George Brett, 3,154
- **Games played:** George Brett, 2,707

CAREER PITCHING LEADERS

- **Wins:** Paul Splittorff, 166
- **Saves:** Jeff Montgomery, 304
- **Strikeouts:** Kevin Appier, 1,458
- **Shutouts:** Dennis Leonard, 23

Kansas City's George Brett chased a .400 batting average in 1980 but settled for .390.

The Royals participated in a parade to honor their 2015 World Series win.

GREATEST SEASONS

The Royals won their second straight AL West title in 1985. Then, after defeating the Toronto Blue Jays in seven games in the ALCS, they faced their cross-state rivals from St. Louis in the World Series. Kansas City took advantage of a blown call by an umpire in the ninth inning of Game 6 to pull out a shocking victory, followed by an 11–0 blowout in Game 7 to win the title.

Thirty years later, the Royals were still looking for their second ring. A core of young, talented players had won the pennant in 2014 but lost a nail-biter in Game 7 of the World Series against the San Francisco Giants. However, the Royals would not be denied in 2015. Now playoff-tested, the young team rolled past the New York Mets in five games to bring the World Series trophy back to Missouri.

TEAM HISTORY

In 1958, the Dodgers were the first MLB team to put down roots in Los Angeles, California. But three years later, the expansion Angels began play in the AL. The teams actually shared Dodger Stadium from 1962 to 1965, but the Angels were already casting their gaze to the south. They opened their new ballpark in Anaheim, California, in 1966. But with only three division titles and no pennants in their first 40 years, the Angels were clearly the No. 2 team in the market. That changed in 2002 when they won their first World Series. Since then, they've routinely drawn more than three million fans to their home games each season as they fight to return to the mountaintop.

Mike Trout has proven to be one of baseball's all-time great players.

GREATEST PLAYERS

- **Garret Anderson**, LF (1994–2008)
- **Brian Downing**, OF-DH (1978–90)
- **Darin Erstad**, OF-1B (1996–2006)
- **Chuck Finley**, LHP (1986–99)
- **Jim Fregosi**, SS (1961–71)
- **Bobby Grich**, IF (1977–86)
- **Shohei Ohtani**, DH-RHP (2018 –)
- **Nolan Ryan**, RHP (1972–79)
- **Tim Salmon**, RF (1992–2004, 2006)
- **Mike Trout**, CF (2011–)

Nolan Ryan threw four no-hitters for the Angels during the 1970s and led the AL in strikeouts seven times.

TEAM STATS AND RECORDS

ALL-TIME RECORD

- **Regular season:** 4,812–4,838
- **Postseason:** 27–37, one World Series title

TOP MANAGERS

- **Bill Rigney** (1961–69); 625–707 (regular season)
- **Mike Scioscia** (2000–18); 1,650–1,428 (regular season); 21–27, one World Series title (postseason)

CAREER BATTING LEADERS

- **Home runs:** Mike Trout, 310
- **RBIs:** Garret Anderson, 1,292
- **Runs:** Garret Anderson, 1,024
- **Hits:** Garret Anderson, 2,368
- **Games played:** Garret Anderson, 2,013

CAREER PITCHING LEADERS

- **Wins:** Chuck Finley, 165
- **Saves:** Troy Percival, 316
- **Strikeouts:** Nolan Ryan, 2,416
- **Shutouts:** Nolan Ryan, 40

MANY MILESTONES

Though they didn't spend the majority of their careers with the Angels, three future Hall of Famers achieved statistical milestones in Angels uniforms. Reggie Jackson hit his 500th career home run on September 17, 1984, against the Kansas City Royals. First baseman Rod Carew collected his 3,000th career hit on August 4, 1985, in a game against his former team, the Minnesota Twins. And pitcher Don Sutton earned his 300th career victory on June 18, 1986, when he beat the Texas Rangers.

GREATEST SEASONS

The Angels have gone by many names over the years—the Los Angeles Angels, the California Angels, the Anaheim Angels, and even the Los Angeles Angels of Anaheim. But they've only been called World Champions once. In 2002, the Angels won 99 games

Chuck Finley lets go of a pitch in 1989. The 6-foot-6 left-hander won a team-record 165 games with the Angels.

but had to settle for the AL's wild-card spot after finishing second to Oakland in the AL West. In the American League Division Series (ALDS), the Angels ousted the Yankees, who had won four straight AL pennants. Then they dumped the Minnesota Twins in five games in the ALCS. Facing the San Francisco Giants in the World Series, the Angels rallied to win Games 6 and 7 at home to give their fans a championship.

TEAM HISTORY

The Dodgers began playing in Brooklyn, New York, in 1884. The team went by many nicknames along the way. Bridegrooms, Superbas, and Robins were among them. Dodgers finally stuck in 1932. While in New York, the team battled the NL's Giants and AL's Yankees for city bragging rights. In 1958, the Dodgers and Giants moved to California, expanding MLB's reach from coast to coast. In Los Angeles, the Dodgers established themselves as one of the NL's best teams. Their rivalry with the Giants continues to this day.

Pee Wee Reese was named an All-Star ten times during his 16 years with the Dodgers.

GREATEST PLAYERS

- **Roy Campanella**, C (1948–57)
- **Don Drysdale**, RHP (1956–69)
- **Orel Hershiser**, RHP (1983–94, 2000)
- **Clayton Kershaw**, LHP (2008–)
- **Sandy Koufax**, LHP (1955–66)
- **Mike Piazza**, C (1992–98)
- **Pee Wee Reese**, SS (1940–42, 1946–58)
- **Jackie Robinson**, 1B-2B (1947–56)
- **Duke Snider**, CF (1947–62)
- **Don Sutton**, RHP (1966–80, 1988)

JACKIE ROBINSON

Jackie Robinson was 28 years old when he broke the MLB color barrier. He batted over .300 in six consecutive seasons and scored more than 100 runs in six of seven years. Robinson also led the NL in stolen bases in 1947 and 1949. But his statistics pale in comparison to the impact he had on US society. The integration of baseball and his dignified handling of the racism he faced helped pave the way for the civil rights movement of the 1950s and 1960s.

TEAM STATS AND RECORDS

ALL-TIME RECORD

- **Regular season:** 11,123–9,891
- **Postseason:** 128–141, seven World Series titles

TOP MANAGERS

- **Walter Alston** (1954–76); 2,040–1,613 (regular season); 23–21, four World Series titles (postseason)
- **Tom Lasorda** (1976–96); 1,599–1,439 (regular season); 31–30, two World Series titles (postseason)

CAREER BATTING LEADERS

- **Home runs:** Duke Snider, 389
- **RBIs:** Duke Snider, 1,271
- **Runs:** Pee Wee Reese, 1,338
- **Hits:** Zack Wheat, 2,804
- **Games played:** Zack Wheat, 2,322

CAREER PITCHING LEADERS

- **Wins:** Don Sutton, 233
- **Saves:** Kenley Jansen, 350
- **Strikeouts:** Don Sutton, 2,696
- **Shutouts:** Don Sutton, 52

Players such as Reed Johnson, *left*, Matt Kemp, *center*, and Andre Ethier helped the Dodgers become contenders again during the 2000s.

The Dodgers rush to congratulate each other after their World Series win on October 27, 2020.

GREATEST SEASONS

The Dodgers have had a number of amazing seasons. But no season was quite like 2020. The season didn't start until late July due to the COVID-19 pandemic. When play finally began, fans weren't allowed in the ballparks. Nonetheless, the Dodgers quickly took control of the NL West. Manager Dave Roberts pushed all the right buttons. Veteran ace Clayton Kershaw led a deep pitching staff. Right fielder Mookie Betts thrived in his first season in Los Angeles.

The Dodgers had made the playoffs in each of the previous seven seasons, but during that period they had only reached the World Series twice and lost both times. This time would be different. With their backs against the wall in the NLCS, they won three straight against the Atlanta Braves to reach the World Series. Then, in a World Series played at a neutral site in Texas, they knocked off the Tampa Bay Rays in six games to win their first title since 1988.

MIAMI MARLINS

TEAM HISTORY

The city of Miami had been trying to get an MLB team for years. Finally, the NL was looking to expand, and the Florida Marlins were born in 1993. They were named for a minor league team that once played in Miami. Team owners chose to identify the team by the state name rather than the city, as it was the only MLB team in Florida at the time.

The Marlins played their games at a converted football stadium. In 1997, Florida won the World Series in just its fifth season. Another title followed in 2003.

In 2012, the team moved into a new, retractable-roof stadium in downtown Miami. They updated their name to the Miami Marlins. More changes happened in 2019, when the team revamped its orange and black colors to blue, red, black, and gray.

GREATEST PLAYERS

- **Miguel Cabrera**, 3B-RF (2003–07)
- **Luis Castillo**, 2B (1996–2005)
- **Jeff Conine**, 1B-OF (1993–97, 2003–05)
- **José Fernández**, RHP (2013–16)
- **Josh Johnson**, RHP (2005–12)
- **Mike Lowell**, 3B (1999–2005)
- **Hanley Ramirez**, SS (2006–12)
- **Gary Sheffield**, RF (1993–98)
- **Giancarlo Stanton**, RF (2010–17)
- **Dontrelle Willis**, LHP (2003–07)

Sandy Alcantara pitches to the Braves during a 2021 game in Miami.

TEAM STATS AND RECORDS

ALL-TIME RECORD

- **Regular season:** 2,088–2,438
- **Postseason:** 24–14, two World Series titles

TOP MANAGERS

- **Jack McKeon** (2003–05, 2011); 281–257 (regular season); 11–6, one World Series title (postseason)
- **Don Mattingly** (2016–); 374–494 (regular season); 0–0 (postseason)

CAREER BATTING LEADERS

- **Home runs:** Giancarlo Stanton, 267
- **RBIs:** Giancarlo Stanton, 672
- **Runs:** Luis Castillo, 675
- **Hits:** Luis Castillo, 1,273
- **Games played:** Luis Castillo, 1,128

CAREER PITCHING LEADERS

- **Wins:** Ricky Nolasco, 81
- **Saves:** Robb Nen, 108
- **Strikeouts:** Ricky Nolasco, 1,001
- **Shutouts:** A. J. Burnett and Dontrelle Willis, 8

With his high leg kick and wicked fastball, rookie pitcher Dontrelle Willis gave the Marlins a big lift in 2003.

Manager Jack McKeon is lifted into the air by his players after the Marlins won the World Series in 2003.

GREATEST SEASONS

The 1997 Marlins won 92 games and earned the wild-card spot in the NL playoffs. They beat the Atlanta Braves in six games to reach the World Series. Then, in a tense, back-and-forth battle against Cleveland, the Marlins won Game 7 when Edgar Rentería singled home Craig Counsell in the 11th inning for a 3–2 victory.

The Marlins were back in the playoffs as a wild card in 2003. They staged a huge comeback to defeat the Chicago Cubs in seven games in the NLCS. Facing a veteran New York Yankees team in the World Series, 23-year-old ace Josh Beckett pitched a five-hit shutout in Game 6 to clinch the Marlins' second title.

REMEMBERING JOSÉ FERNÁNDEZ

Right-hander José Fernández appeared to be on his way to an outstanding career. He won the NL Rookie of the Year Award in 2013. After coming back from an arm injury, he made his second NL All-Star team in 2016. But tragedy struck that September when Fernández was killed in a boating accident. He was just 24 years old.

TEAM HISTORY

The Seattle Pilots played their only season in 1969. They lost 98 games and finished last in the AL West. The owners couldn't pay the bills, so they were forced to sell. The new owners moved the team to Milwaukee, Wisconsin, which had been home to the Braves from 1953 to 1965. For the next few decades, the Milwaukee Brewers spent most of their time near the bottom of the division. In 1998, they moved to the NL as part of divisional realignment.

Relief pitcher Josh Hader prepares to deliver a pitch in a 2021 game.

Robin Yount was the Brewers' starting shortstop in 1974 as an 18-year-old rookie.

GREATEST PLAYERS

- **Hank Aaron**, DH (1975–76)
- **Ryan Braun**, 3B-OF (2007–2020)
- **Mike Caldwell**, LHP (1977–84)
- **Cecil Cooper**, 1B (1977–87)
- **Prince Fielder**, 1B (2005–2011)
- **Rollie Fingers**, RHP (1981–82, 1984–85)

- **Yovani Gallardo**, RHP (2007–14)
- **Teddy Higuera**, LHP (1985–91, 1993–94)
- **Paul Molitor**, 2B-3B-DH (1978–92)
- **Ben Oglivie**, OF (1978–86)
- **Robin Yount**, SS-OF (1974–93)

Milwaukee players celebrate on April 20, 1987. The Brewers had just beaten the host White Sox 5–4 to improve to 13–0.

TEAM STATS AND RECORDS

ALL-TIME RECORD

- **Regular season:** 4,037–4,315
- **Postseason:** 21–28

TOP MANAGERS

- **Phil Garner** (1992–99); 563–617 (regular season)
- **Ned Yost** (2003–08); 457–502 (regular season)

CAREER BATTING LEADERS

- **Home runs:** Ryan Braun, 352
- **RBIs:** Robin Yount, 1,406
- **Runs:** Robin Yount, 1,632
- **Hits:** Robin Yount, 3,142
- **Games played:** Robin Yount, 2,856

CAREER PITCHING LEADERS

- **Wins:** Jim Slaton, 117
- **Saves:** Dan Plesac, 133
- **Strikeouts:** Yovani Gallardo, 1,226
- **Shutouts:** Jim Slaton, 19

GREATEST SEASONS

The Brewers had the AL East's best record in a strike-shortened 1981 season. The team made its first playoff appearance that year, but it lost to the New York Yankees in the divisional round. However, the next year would be a remarkable one. Shortstop Robin Yount won the AL MVP Award. Right-hander Pete Vuckovich was the AL Cy Young winner. And the Brewers took the AL East crown when Don Sutton shut down the Orioles in Baltimore on the last day of the regular season.

Milwaukee faced the Angels in the ALCS. After losing the first two games on the road, the Brewers stormed back to sweep the next three at home and win the series. The World Series against the Cardinals lasted seven games. Milwaukee won three of the first five, but back home in St. Louis, the Cardinals took the last two to deny the Brewers their first title.

FIFTY HOME RUNS

In 2007, Brewers first baseman Prince Fielder became the youngest major league player to hit 50 home runs in a season. He was 23 years old. Fielder finished the 2007 season with an even 50, breaking the Brewers record of 45 shared by Gorman Thomas in 1979 and Richie Sexson in 2001 and 2003.

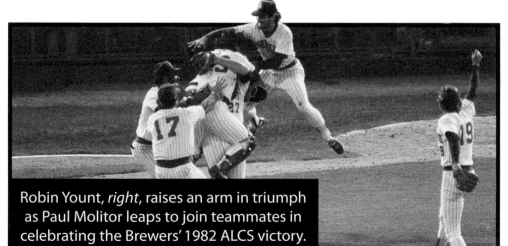

Robin Yount, *right*, raises an arm in triumph as Paul Molitor leaps to join teammates in celebrating the Brewers' 1982 ALCS victory.

MINNESOTA TWINS

TEAM HISTORY

The Washington Senators were founding members of the AL in 1901. However, they weren't very good. They won just three pennants and one World Series in 60 years. In 1961, their owners moved them to the Twin Cities in Minnesota. Soon the newly named Twins were atop the AL. They won the pennant in 1965 and AL West titles in 1969 and 1970. Many lean years followed. The Twins moved into a domed stadium in downtown Minneapolis in 1982 and won two World Series there. But the Metrodome proved to be a tough sell for Minnesotans, who like to spend their summers outdoors. When Target Field opened in 2010, it was widely regarded as one of the best ballparks in MLB. However, the Twins had a tough time putting a championship team on the field. Through 2021 Minnesota had lost an MLB record of 18 straight playoff games.

Kirby Puckett gets ready to swing during a 1994 game against the Oakland Athletics.

Max Kepler slams a home run in a 2021 game against the White Sox.

GREATEST PLAYERS

- **Bert Blyleven**, RHP (1970–76, 1985–88)
- **Rod Carew**, 2B-1B (1967–78)
- **Kent Hrbek**, 1B (1981–94)
- **Walter Johnson**, SP (1907–27)
- **Harmon Killebrew**, 3B-1B (1954–74)
- **Joe Mauer**, C-1B (2004–18)
- **Justin Morneau**, 1B (2003–13)
- **Tony Oliva**, OF-DH (1962–76)
- **Kirby Puckett**, OF (1984–1995)
- **Sam Rice**, OF (1915–33)

TEAM STATS AND RECORDS

ALL-TIME RECORD

- **Regular season:** 9,012–9,716
- **Postseason:** 33–56, three World Series titles

TOP MANAGERS

- **Bucky Harris** (1924–28, 1935–42, 1950–54); 1,336–1,416 (regular season); 7–7, one World Series title (postseason)
- **Tom Kelly** (1986–2001); 1,140–1,244 (regular season); 16–8, two World Series titles (postseason)

CAREER BATTING LEADERS

- **Home runs:** Harmon Killebrew, 559
- **RBIs:** Harmon Killebrew, 1,540
- **Runs:** Sam Rice, 1,466
- **Hits:** Sam Rice, 2,889
- **Games played:** Harmon Killebrew, 2,329

CAREER PITCHING LEADERS

- **Wins:** Walter Johnson, 417
- **Saves:** Joe Nathan, 260
- **Strikeouts:** Walter Johnson, 3,509
- **Shutouts:** Walter Johnson, 110

GREATEST SEASONS

The Twins caught fire in 1987. They used the quirky dimensions and springy turf of the Metrodome to go 56–25 at home during the regular season. That was enough to win the AL West. Then they won all six home postseason games against the Detroit Tigers and St. Louis Cardinals to clinch their first World Series. They were back at it four years later, this time with 51 home victories in the regular season. They also had a great postseason as they defeated the Toronto Blue Jays and Atlanta Braves for their second ring.

JOE MAUER

Playing catcher is one of the toughest jobs in sports. Most catchers aren't expected to be great hitters due to the physical demands of the position. Joe Mauer proved otherwise. The St. Paul, Minnesota, native won the AL batting title in his third major league season, batting .347 in 2006. He won it again in 2008, batting .328. Mauer won it once more in 2009, batting .365. That was the highest single-season average by a catcher in major league history. He also hit 28 home runs in 2009, got on base in almost half of his plate appearances, and won the AL MVP Award.

Joe Mauer, *left*, and Justin Morneau were nicknamed the "M&M Boys." Morneau was the AL MVP in 2006, and Mauer matched the feat in 2009.

TEAM HISTORY

After the 1957 season, both of New York's NL teams—the New York Giants and the Brooklyn Dodgers—moved to California. That left a big hole in the hearts of baseball fans in the country's most populated city. It would be filled by an expansion club that started in 1962. The New York Mets wore the blue of the Dodgers and the orange of the Giants, hoping to unify the former rival fans. They played their first two seasons at the Polo Grounds, the Giants' old ballpark. Then Shea Stadium opened in Queens, roughly midway between the Polo Grounds and Ebbets Field in Brooklyn.

Jacob deGrom won back-to-back NL Cy Young Awards in 2018 and 2019.

The Mets were known as lovable losers in those early days. Then the "Amazin' Mets" came out of nowhere to win the World Series in 1969. They found their footing and began to compete with the Yankees for the attention of New York baseball fans. In 2009, the team moved to Citi Field, next to the site of old Shea Stadium.

GREATEST PLAYERS

- **Carlos Beltrán**, CF (2005–11)
- **Jacob deGrom**, RHP (2014–)
- **John Franco**, LHP (1990–2001, 2003–04)
- **Dwight Gooden**, RHP (1984–94)
- **Keith Hernandez**, 1B (1983–89)
- **Jerry Koosman**, LHP (1967–78)
- **Mike Piazza**, C (1998–2005)
- **Tom Seaver**, RHP (1967–77, 1983)
- **Darryl Strawberry**, RF (1983–90)
- **David Wright**, 3B (2004–16, 2018)

The Mets and their fans at Shea Stadium rejoice after the team won the 1969 World Series in five games over the Orioles.

TEAM STATS AND RECORDS

ALL-TIME RECORD
- **Regular season:** 4,551–4,927
- **Postseason:** 51–38, two World Series titles

TOP MANAGERS
- **Davey Johnson** (1984–90); 595–417 (regular season); 11–9, one World Series title (postseason)
- **Terry Collins** (2011–17); 551–583 (regular season); 8–7 (postseason)

CAREER BATTING LEADERS
- **Home runs:** Darryl Strawberry, 252
- **RBIs:** David Wright, 970
- **Runs:** David Wright, 949
- **Hits:** David Wright, 1,777
- **Games played:** Ed Kranepool, 1,853

CAREER PITCHING LEADERS
- **Wins:** Tom Seaver, 198
- **Saves:** John Franco, 276
- **Strikeouts:** Tom Seaver, 2,541
- **Shutouts:** Tom Seaver, 44

Darryl Strawberry watches his solo home run in the Mets' victory over the Astros in Game 5 of the 1986 NLCS.

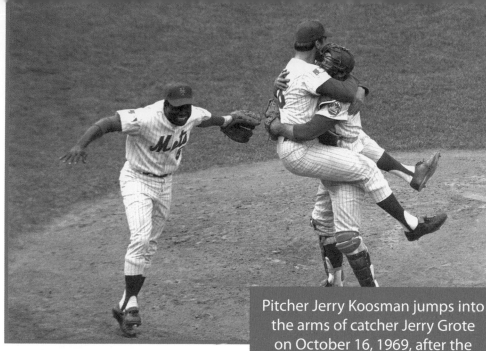

Pitcher Jerry Koosman jumps into the arms of catcher Jerry Grote on October 16, 1969, after the Mets won their first World Series.

GREATEST SEASONS

After posting seven straight losing seasons—and averaging 105 losses per year along the way—the Mets provided little reason to expect a sudden turnaround in 1969. Instead, they played respectable baseball. By mid-August they were 11 games over .500, but they were still ten games behind the first-place Chicago Cubs.

Then the Mets got red-hot. They won 38 of their last 49 games to take the NL East title. After sweeping the Atlanta Braves in the NLCS, they shocked the mighty Baltimore Orioles to win the World Series in five games.

WINNING THE 1986 WORLD SERIES

In the 1986 World Series, the Mets trailed the Boston Red Sox 5–3 in the tenth inning of Game 6. Boston needed just three outs to win the title. The first two batters were retired. A Red Sox victory seemed all but certain. But three straight singles and a wild pitch tied the game. Then a Boston error on Mookie Wilson's ground ball gave the Mets the winning run. Two nights later, the Mets won Game 7 to win their second World Series.

TEAM HISTORY

The Yankees began as the New York Highlanders in 1903. Ten years later, they changed their name to the Yankees. But their fortunes didn't soar until they got the great Babe Ruth from the Boston Red Sox in 1920. Starting in 1921, they won six of the next eight AL pennants and three World Series. That was the start of baseball's greatest dynasty. No team has won more World Series than the Yankees. And more Hall of Famers have played for the Yankees than for any other team. The New York Yankees are considered the greatest team in MLB history for a good reason.

Many baseball experts still consider Babe Ruth, who hit 714 career home runs, the greatest player in the sport's history.

Aaron Judge, *center*, and Tim Locastro, *left*, congratulate each other on beating the Mets in a July 2021 game.

GREATEST PLAYERS

- **Yogi Berra**, C (1946–63)
- **Joe DiMaggio**, CF (1936–42, 1946–51)
- **Whitey Ford**, LHP (1950, 1953–67)
- **Lou Gehrig**, 1B (1923–39)
- **Derek Jeter**, SS (1995–2014)
- **Mickey Mantle**, CF (1951–68)
- **Don Mattingly**, 1B (1982–95)
- **Thurman Munson**, C (1969–79)
- **Mariano Rivera**, RHP (1995–2013)
- **Babe Ruth**, RF (1920–34)

DEREK JETER

No recent Yankees player is more recognizable than Derek Jeter. The shortstop was the AL Rookie of the Year in 1996. He helped lead the Yankees to World Series wins in four of his first five seasons. He retired in 2014 as the team's all-time leader in games played, hits, doubles, and stolen bases. In 158 career postseason games, Jeter hit .308 with 200 hits and 20 home runs.

TEAM STATS AND RECORDS

ALL-TIME RECORD

- **Regular season:** 10,503–7,937
- **Postseason:** 241–172, 27 World Series titles

TOP MANAGERS

- **Joe McCarthy** (1931–46); 1,460–867 (regular season); 29–9, seven World Series titles (postseason)
- **Joe Torre** (1996–2007); 1,173–767 (regular season); 76–47, four World Series titles (postseason)

CAREER BATTING LEADERS

- **Home runs:** Babe Ruth, 659
- **RBIs:** Lou Gehrig, 1,995
- **Runs:** Babe Ruth, 1,959
- **Hits:** Derek Jeter, 3,465
- **Games played:** Derek Jeter, 2,747

CAREER PITCHING LEADERS

- **Wins:** Whitey Ford, 236
- **Saves:** Mariano Rivera, 652
- **Strikeouts:** Andy Pettitte, 2,020
- **Shutouts:** Whitey Ford, 45

Mickey Mantle entered the Baseball Hall of Fame in 1974.

Shortstop Derek Jeter, *center*, and closer Mariano Rivera, *right*, smile after beating the Phillies to win the 2009 World Series.

GREATEST SEASONS

It's hard to pick even a greatest era for a team with the Yankees' track record of success. From the 1920s to today, the Yankees won multiple World Series in every decade except the 1980s and 2010s. But in 1996, a bit of tarnish had begun to show on the Yankees' crown. It had been 18 years since their last World Series victory. However, a core of outstanding young players had begun to assemble. Shortstop Derek Jeter, center fielder Bernie Williams, left-handed starting pitcher Andy Pettitte, and reliever Mariano Rivera helped restore the shine that year. The Yankees cruised through the AL playoffs. Then, after dropping the first two games of the World Series to the Atlanta Braves, they swept the next four to take the title. That was the first of four World Series victories in five seasons for the Yankees.

TEAM HISTORY

Founded in Philadelphia in 1901, the Athletics—or A's, as they're frequently called—were one of the AL's early powers. Between 1905 and 1914, they won five pennants and three World Series. They also had a three-year run atop the league from 1929 to 1931. But the NL's Phillies were more popular with the hometown fans. In 1955, the A's moved to Kansas City. After 13 losing seasons, they moved

again. This time they went to Oakland, California. And that's where the A's finally became consistent winners. Wearing their trademark green and gold uniforms, the A's won five straight AL West titles from 1971 to 1975. They also won three straight World Series. The A's established themselves as a worthy rival to the Giants for Bay Area baseball supremacy.

Rickey Henderson steals third base in a 1982 game in Oakland.

GREATEST PLAYERS

- **Sal Bando**, 3B (1966–76)
- **Bert Campaneris**, SS (1964–76)
- **Jose Canseco**, OF (1985–92, 1997)
- **Dennis Eckersley**, RHP (1987–95)
- **Rollie Fingers**, RHP (1968–76)
- **Jimmie Foxx**, 1B-3B-C (1925–35)
- **Lefty Grove**, LHP (1925–33)
- **Rickey Henderson**, OF (1979–84, 1989–93, 1994–95, 1998)
- **Jim Hunter**, RHP (1965–74)
- **Eddie Plank**, LHP (1901–14)

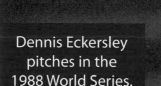

Dennis Eckersley pitches in the 1988 World Series.

TEAM STATS AND RECORDS

ALL-TIME RECORD

- **Regular season:** 9,150–9,552
- **Postseason:** 85–82, nine World Series titles

TOP MANAGERS

- **Connie Mack** (1901–50); 3,582–3,814 (regular season); 24–19, five World Series titles (postseason)
- **Tony La Russa** (1986–95); 798–673 (regular season); 19–12, one World Series title (postseason)

CAREER BATTING LEADERS

- **Home runs:** Mark McGwire, 363
- **RBIs:** Al Simmons, 1,179
- **Runs:** Rickey Henderson, 1,270
- **Hits:** Bert Campaneris, 1,882
- **Games played:** Bert Campaneris, 1,795

CAREER PITCHING LEADERS

- **Wins:** Eddie Plank, 284
- **Saves:** Dennis Eckersley, 320
- **Strikeouts:** Eddie Plank, 1,985
- **Shutouts:** Eddie Plank, 59

Elvis Andrus watches the ball fly in the eighth inning of a 2021 game against the Red Sox.

Dave Parker, *right*, gets congratulated by Dave Henderson after hitting a home run during Game 1 of the 1989 World Series.

GREATEST SEASONS

The 1988 Athletics won 104 games and rolled to the AL pennant. But they were shocked by the underdog Los Angeles Dodgers in the World Series. The next year, led by sluggers José Canseco and Mark McGwire and ace closer Dennis Eckersley, the Athletics again cruised to the World Series. Facing the rival Giants, a deadly earthquake struck as Game 3 was about to start. After a week's delay, the series resumed and a four-game sweep earned the Athletics their long-awaited title.

THE UNBEATABLE ATHLETICS

For three weeks in 2002, the Athletics were unbeatable. From August 13 to September 4, the club got 20 straight wins. This was an MLB record at the time. The Athletics started the streak in third place in the AL West, 4.5 games out of first. When the streak ended, they were in first place by 3.5 games. The final three games in the streak were walk-off victories, including the 20th on a pinch-hit home run by Scott Hatteberg to beat Kansas City. The Athletics ended up winning 103 games and the West Division title, though they were upset by the Minnesota Twins in the ALDS.

TEAM HISTORY

In 1883, the Philadelphia Phillies began playing in the NL. The team wasn't very successful in its early days. It won just one NL pennant in its first 67 years of play. The 1950 team made a surprise run to the World Series, but it wasn't until the mid-1970s that the Phillies became a consistent playoff presence. They suffered crushing defeats in the NLCS in 1976, 1977, and 1978. But in 1980 it all came together, and the Phillies won their first World Series. In 2004, they moved into Citizens Bank Park. This was a modern ballpark with a retro feel. Four years later they won their second title.

Jean Segura hits a two-run single during a July 2021 game against the Cubs.

Phillies pitcher Robin Roberts is shown on October 3, 1950, preparing for the World Series against the Yankees. The Philadelphia team surprised many baseball followers by reaching the Series that year.

GREATEST PLAYERS

- **Pete Alexander**, RHP (1911–17, 1930)
- **Dick Allen**, 1B-3B-OF (1963–69, 1975–76)
- **Richie Ashburn**, CF (1948–59)
- **Steve Carlton**, LHP (1972–86)

- **Cole Hamels**, LHP (2006–15)
- **Bryce Harper**, RF (2019–)
- **Robin Roberts**, RHP (1948–61)
- **Jimmy Rollins**, SS (2000–14)
- **Mike Schmidt**, 3B (1972–89)
- **Chase Utley**, 2B (2003–15)

TEAM STATS AND RECORDS

ALL-TIME RECORD
- **Regular season:** 9,935–11,112
- **Postseason:** 49–54, two World Series titles

TOP MANAGERS
- **Gene Mauch** (1960–68); 646–684 (regular season)
- **Charlie Manuel** (2005–13); 780–636 (regular season); 27–19, one World Series title (postseason)

CAREER BATTING LEADERS
- **Home runs:** Mike Schmidt, 548
- **RBIs:** Mike Schmidt, 1,595
- **Runs:** Mike Schmidt, 1,506
- **Hits:** Jimmy Rollins, 2,306
- **Games played:** Mike Schmidt, 2,404

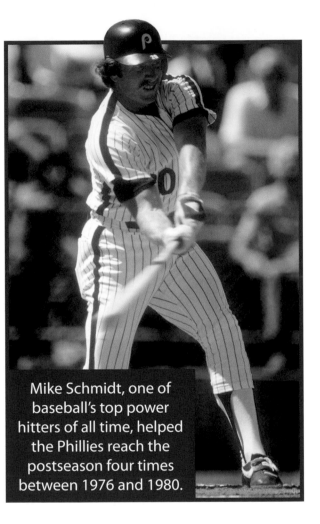

Mike Schmidt, one of baseball's top power hitters of all time, helped the Phillies reach the postseason four times between 1976 and 1980.

CAREER PITCHING LEADERS
- **Wins:** Steve Carlton, 241
- **Saves:** Jonathan Papelbon, 123
- **Strikeouts:** Steve Carlton, 3,031
- **Shutouts:** Pete Alexander, 61

GREATEST SEASONS

Heading into the last weekend of the 1980 season, the Phillies and Montreal Expos were tied for first place in the NL East. The teams faced off in a three-game series in Montreal to decide the division title. After a 2–1 win on Friday night, the Phillies got a two-run homer from Mike Schmidt in the 11th inning on Saturday to clinch the division.

The Phillies needed extra innings to beat the Houston Astros in the final two games of the NLCS. This sent Philadelphia to the World Series for the first time since 1950. The Kansas City Royals were no match. The Phillies won it in six games to give their fans their first World Series title.

In 2008, the team took over first place in late September and rolled through the playoffs. They lost only three games in three series. The Phillies defeated the Tampa Bay Rays in five games to take another title.

PHILLIES MASCOT

The Phillie Phanatic is one of the most recognizable mascots in all of sports. The fuzzy, green, flightless bird has been entertaining fans at Phillies games since 1978.

Philadelphia's Cole Hamels pitches during Game 5 of the 2008 World Series.

TEAM HISTORY

The Pirates' history traces back to a team called the Pittsburgh Alleghenys, who played in the American Association from 1882 to 1886. In 1887, they jumped to the rival NL. By 1891, they had become the Pirates. Starting in 1901, the team won three straight NL pennants. In 1903, it accepted a challenge from AL champion Boston to a postseason showdown. That's now known as the first World Series. The Pirates have had a number of strong eras, most notably the 1970s, when they won two titles.

The Pirates' Barry Bonds belts a home run in 1990 against the Cubs. Bonds had 33 homers, 114 RBIs, and 52 stolen bases that year.

A RARE BASEBALL CARD

A card that shows the Pirates' Honus Wagner went on to become the most expensive baseball card of all time. The rare card was printed in 1909 by a cigarette company. Wagner was opposed to smoking, so he asked the company to stop printing the cards. That limited the number produced, making them more valuable. One of the cards sold for $3.25 million in 2020.

Gregory Polanco takes a swing during an August 2021 game against the Brewers.

GREATEST PLAYERS

- **Barry Bonds**, LF (1986–92)
- **Roberto Clemente**, RF (1955–72)
- **Ralph Kiner**, LF (1946–53)
- **Bill Mazeroski**, 2B (1956–72)
- **Andrew McCutchen**, CF (2009–17)
- **Dave Parker**, RF (1973–83)

- **Willie Stargell**, OF-1B (1962–82)
- **Pie Traynor**, 3B (1920–35, 1937)
- **Arky Vaughan**, SS (1932–41)
- **Honus Wagner**, SS (1900–17)
- **Paul Waner**, RF (1926–40)

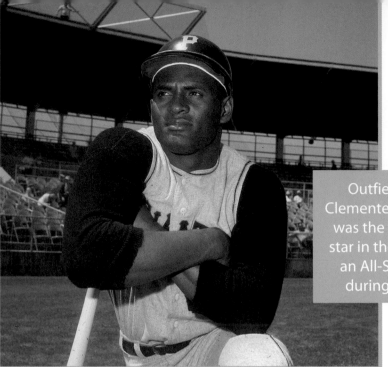

Outfielder Roberto Clemente, shown in 1968, was the Pirates' biggest star in the 1960s. He was an All-Star nine times during that decade.

TEAM STATS AND RECORDS

ALL-TIME RECORD

- **Regular season:** 10,625–10,547
- **Postseason:** 43–54, five World Series titles

TOP MANAGERS

- **Fred Clarke** (1900–15); 1,422–969 (regular season); 7–8, one World Series title (postseason)
- **Danny Murtaugh** (1957–64, 1967, 1970–71, 1973–76); 1,115–950 (regular season); 12–16, two World Series titles (postseason)

CAREER BATTING LEADERS

- **Home runs:** Willie Stargell, 475
- **RBIs:** Willie Stargell, 1,540
- **Runs:** Honus Wagner, 1,521
- **Hits:** Roberto Clemente, 3,000
- **Games played:** Roberto Clemente and Honus Wagner, 2,433

CAREER PITCHING LEADERS

- **Wins:** Wilbur Cooper, 202
- **Saves:** Roy Face, 186
- **Strikeouts:** Bob Friend, 1,682
- **Shutouts:** Babe Adams, 44

GREATEST SEASONS

The 1960 Pirates were a special team. Pittsburgh had terrific defense all around the diamond. Vernon Law, who won 20 games and the Cy Young Award, led the pitching staff. Right fielder Roberto Clemente hit .314 with 94 RBIs. Meanwhile shortstop Dick Groat was the NL MVP after leading the league with a .325 batting average. These players helped the Pirates cruise to the NL pennant.

Pittsburgh met the mighty Yankees in the World Series. New York won three of the first six games in a blowout fashion. But the Pirates pulled out three close wins of their own. Game 7 in Pittsburgh went back and forth. Pittsburgh scored five runs in the eighth to take a 9–7 lead. The Yankees tied it in the top of the ninth. But second baseman Bill Mazeroski led off the bottom of the inning with one of the most dramatic home runs in World Series history. This gave the Pirates a 10–9 victory and the championship.

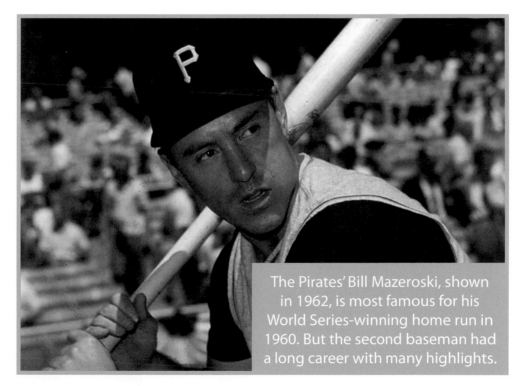

The Pirates' Bill Mazeroski, shown in 1962, is most famous for his World Series-winning home run in 1960. But the second baseman had a long career with many highlights.

TEAM HISTORY

San Diego, California, was home to a minor league team called the Padres starting in 1936. San Diego native Ted Williams, a future Hall of Famer with the Boston Red Sox, was one of their earliest stars. The Padres played in the Pacific Coast League (PCL). It was considered the top minor league circuit in the country. But when fellow PCL cities Los Angeles and San Francisco got their own major league teams in 1958, their neighbor to the south wanted in on the action. In 1969, the Padres were welcomed to the NL. The club has had a rough go of it at times. But playing at beautiful Petco Park, they've shown that San Diego remains a great baseball city.

GREATEST PLAYERS

- **Nate Colbert**, INF-OF (1969–74)
- **Rollie Fingers**, RP (1977–80)
- **Steve Garvey**, 1B (1983–87)
- **Tony Gwynn**, RF (1982–2001)
- **Trevor Hoffman**, RHP (1993–2008)
- **Randy Jones**, LHP (1973–80)
- **Manny Machado**, 3B (2019–)
- **Jake Peavy**, RHP (2002–09)
- **Fernando Tatis Jr.**, SS (2019–)
- **Dave Winfield**, RF (1973–80)

Fernando Tatis Jr. watches his home run during a 2021 game against the Oakland Athletics.

TEAM STATS AND RECORDS

ALL-TIME RECORD

- **Regular season:** 3,863–4,495
- **Postseason:** 14–26

TOP MANAGERS

- **Bruce Bochy** (1995–2006); 951–975 (regular season); 8–16 (postseason)
- **Bud Black** (2007–15); 649–713 (regular season)

CAREER BATTING LEADERS

- **Home runs:** Nate Colbert, 163
- **RBIs:** Tony Gwynn, 1,138
- **Runs:** Tony Gwynn, 1,383
- **Hits:** Tony Gwynn, 3,141
- **Games played:** Tony Gwynn, 2,440

CAREER PITCHING LEADERS

- **Wins:** Eric Show, 100
- **Saves:** Trevor Hoffman, 552
- **Strikeouts:** Jake Peavy, 1,348
- **Shutouts:** Randy Jones, 18

Tony Gwynn follows through on a swing during a 1994 game.

GREATEST SEASONS

The Padres' lone postseason appearance in their first 27 years came in 1984. After winning eight of their first nine games, they took over first place in the NL West in early June. They stayed there the rest of the way. Young outfielder Tony Gwynn hit .351. Veterans Steve Garvey and Graig Nettles anchored the corner infield spots. They brought playoff experience from their days with the Dodgers and Yankees, respectively. Intimidating closer Goose Gossage—another former Yankees star—keyed a strong bullpen.

In the NLCS against the Chicago Cubs, the Padres lost the first two games at Wrigley Field. But back in San Diego, the Padres responded in a big way. After a 7–1 victory in Game 3, they took Game 4 on Garvey's two-run homer in the bottom of the ninth. Then a four-run seventh inning gave them a 6–3 win in the decisive Game 5.

Alan Wiggins slides home during the 1984 World Series against the Tigers.

A dominant Detroit Tigers team proved to be too much to handle in the World Series. But Padres fans will always remember their first time on MLB's biggest stage.

ALMOST REACHING THE RECORD

The 1994 players' strike may have robbed Tony Gwynn of the chance to become the first player to hit .400 since Ted Williams did it in 1941. Gwynn was hitting .394 when the strike ended the season in August.

TEAM HISTORY

The Giants began play as the NL's New York Gothams in 1883. Two years later, they changed their name to the Giants. One of the league's dominant teams in MLB's early days, the Giants won ten NL pennants from 1905 to 1924. In 1958, owner Horace Stoneham moved the team to San Francisco. California baseball proved to be a hit, and so were the Giants, who had some of the biggest stars in the game in the 1960s. They later built an iconic ballpark on the San Francisco waterfront. The team won three World Series between 2010 and 2014.

First baseman Willie McCovey played 19 seasons with the Giants. He led the NL in home runs three times and was the 1969 NL MVP.

Bill Terry, *right*, and Mel Ott were two of the great Giants players of the 1920s and 1930s. Both later became managers of the team.

GREATEST PLAYERS

- **Barry Bonds**, LF (1993–2007)
- **Madison Bumgarner**, LHP (2009–19)
- **Orlando Cepeda**, 1B-OF (1958–66)
- **Carl Hubbell**, LHP (1928–43)
- **Juan Marichal**, RHP (1960–73)
- **Christy Mathewson**, RHP (1900–16)
- **Willie Mays**, CF (1951–52, 1954–72)
- **Willie McCovey**, 1B (1959–73, 1977–80)
- **Mel Ott**, RF (1926–47)
- **Buster Posey**, C (2009–19, 2021–)

ALL-STAR GAME

The 1934 All-Star Game was at the New York Giants' home field, the Polo Grounds. Giants pitcher Carl Hubbell put on a legendary All-Star Game performance for the crowd. Hubbell struck out five consecutive Hall of Famers with his screwball, which darts the opposite way of a curveball. He fanned Babe Ruth, Lou Gehrig, and Jimmie Foxx to end the first inning. Then he struck out Al Simmons and Joe Cronin to start the second.

TEAM STATS AND RECORDS

ALL-TIME RECORD

- **Regular season:** 11,301–9,773
- **Postseason:** 100–93, eight World Series titles

TOP MANAGERS

- **John McGraw** (1902–32); 2,583–1,790 (regular season); 26–28, three World Series titles (postseason)
- **Bruce Bochy** (2007–19); 1,052–1,054 (regular season); 36–17, three World Series titles (postseason)

CAREER BATTING LEADERS

- **Home runs:** Willie Mays, 646
- **RBIs:** Mel Ott, 1,860
- **Runs:** Willie Mays, 2,011
- **Hits:** Willie Mays, 3,187
- **Games played:** Willie Mays, 2,857

CAREER PITCHING LEADERS

- **Wins:** Christy Mathewson, 372
- **Saves:** Robb Nen, 206
- **Strikeouts:** Christy Mathewson, 2,504
- **Shutouts:** Christy Mathewson, 79

Orlando Cepeda helped turn the San Francisco Giants into a winning team. He was the 1958 NL Rookie of the Year.

Wilmer Flores, *left*, celebrates with Mike Yastrzemski after scoring against the Cardinals in a 2021 game.

GREATEST SEASONS

The Giants began 2014 looking for their third World Series in five years. They stumbled a bit during the regular season but still qualified for the playoffs as a wild card. That's when Madison Bumgarner went to work. The lefty had gone 18–10 in the regular season, but he saved his best for the playoffs. He shut out the Pittsburgh Pirates in the NL wild-card game. He beat the St. Louis Cardinals in the NLCS. Then he knocked down the Kansas City Royals twice in the first five games of the World Series, allowing one run in 16 innings. In Game 7, Bumgarner came out of the bullpen in the fifth inning to protect a 3–2 lead. He blanked the Royals the rest of the way to earn the save and give the Giants another title.

TEAM HISTORY

Seattle, Washington, was home to the Pilots in 1969. However, after one season the team moved to Milwaukee. Civic leaders thought a domed stadium would help increase attendance in rainy Seattle. When the Kingdome was built in the 1970s, the AL agreed to give the city another chance. The Mariners began play as one of two AL expansion teams in 1977. There hasn't been a lot to celebrate over the years. They made four playoff appearances between

Ken Griffey Jr. follows through on his swing at the 1990 All-Star Game at Wrigley Field in Chicago. The young player was known as "The Kid."

1995 and 2001 and have never reached the World Series. But some of the game's biggest stars have played for the Mariners. The Kingdome's replacement, Safeco Field, was also a pioneer among retractable-roof stadiums when it opened in 1999. After the 2018 season it was renamed T-Mobile Park.

GREATEST PLAYERS

- **Jay Buhner**, OF (1988–2001)
- **Alvin Davis**, 1B (1984–91)
- **Ken Griffey Jr.**, CF (1989–99, 2009–10)
- **Félix Hernández**, RHP (2005–19)
- **Randy Johnson**, SP (1989–98)
- **Mark Langston**, SP (1984–89)
- **Edgar Martinez**, 3B-DH (1987–2004)
- **Jamie Moyer**, LHP (1996–2006)
- **Alex Rodriguez**, SS (1994–2000)
- **Ichiro Suzuki**, OF (2001–2012, 2018–19)

Mariners designated hitter Edgar Martinez tips his hat to the crowd during "Edgar Martinez Day" in 2004.

TEAM STATS AND RECORDS

ALL-TIME RECORD
- **Regular season:** 3,336–3,727
- **Postseason:** 15–19

TOP MANAGERS
- **Lou Piniella** (1993–2002); 840–711 (regular season); 15–19 (postseason)
- **Scott Servais** (2016–); 438–432 (regular season)

CAREER BATTING LEADERS
- **Home runs:** Ken Griffey Jr., 417
- **RBIs:** Edgar Martinez, 1,261
- **Runs:** Edgar Martinez, 1,219
- **Hits:** Ichiro Suzuki, 2,542
- **Games played:** Edgar Martinez, 2,055

CAREER PITCHING LEADERS
- **Wins:** Félix Hernández, 169
- **Saves:** Kazuhiro Sasaki, 129
- **Strikeouts:** Félix Hernández, 2,524
- **Shutouts:** Randy Johnson, 19

HONORING EDGAR MARTINEZ

When popular designated hitter Edgar Martinez retired after the 2004 season, his 18 years of service with the Seattle Mariners was honored in an unusual way. The city of Seattle named a street after him. South Atlantic Street was renamed Edgar Martinez Drive. Martinez finished his career with 309 home runs, 1,261 RBIs, and a batting average of .312. A seven-time All-Star, Martinez was presented with the Roberto Clemente Award for his humanitarian service to the community. Following his retirement, MLB also named the award given annually to its best designated hitter after him.

J. P. Crawford attempts to turn a double play in a 2021 game against the Rangers.

GREATEST SEASONS

The 2001 Mariners were one of the greatest teams in MLB history. They tied the 1906 Chicago Cubs for the most wins in a season with 116. Outfielder Ichiro Suzuki arrived from Japan that year and hit .350 to win the AL batting title. He also stole 56 bases. Those stats helped earn him AL MVP and Rookie of the Year honors. Suzuki was joined by second baseman Bret Boone, first baseman John Olerud, and designated hitter Edgar Martinez as starters at the MLB All-Star Game, which was played in Seattle. Boone finished third in MVP voting after hitting .331 with 37 homers and 141 RBIs. Five starting pitchers won at least ten games, and closer Kazuhiro Sasaki posted 45 saves. However, after edging Cleveland in the ALDS, the Mariners lost to the Yankees in the ALCS. Through 2021 they hadn't been back to the playoffs since.

Nolan Arenado races past third base in the seventh inning of a 2021 game against the Giants.

TEAM HISTORY

The St. Louis Browns were one of the top teams in the American Association from 1882 to 1891. They joined the NL in 1892. They changed their name to the Cardinals in 1900 and went on to win more World Series titles than any other NL team. The Cardinals are known for playing a fast-paced brand of ball. But sluggers such as Stan Musial, Mark McGwire, and Albert Pujols put more than their share of balls in the seats too.

YEAR OF THE PITCHER

Bob Gibson achieved arguably the greatest pitching season in history in 1968. In what was known as the Year of the Pitcher for the sensational performances on the mound, Gibson was the best of all. He compiled the lowest ERA ever at the time, at 1.12. And he did so while winning 22 games and striking out 268 batters. His dominance—and that of several other pitchers that season—motivated MLB to lower the mound in 1969 to give batters a better chance and to create more offense in the game.

GREATEST PLAYERS

- **Lou Brock**, LF (1964–79)
- **Dizzy Dean**, P (1930, 1932–37)
- **Curt Flood**, CF (1958–69)
- **Bob Gibson**, SP (1959–75)
- **Rogers Hornsby**, OF (1915–26, 1933)
- **Yadier Molina**, C (2004–)
- **Stan Musial**, OF (1941–44, 1946–63)
- **Albert Pujols**, 1B (2001–11)
- **Enos Slaughter**, OF (1938–42, 1946–53)
- **Ozzie Smith**, SS (1982–96)

Slugger Stan Musial was a three-time MVP and was runner-up four times.

TEAM STATS AND RECORDS

ALL-TIME RECORD

- **Regular season:** 11,038–10,163
- **Postseason:** 134–126, 11 World Series titles

TOP MANAGERS

- **Red Schoendienst** (1965–76, 1980, 1990); 1,041–955 (regular season); 7–7, one World Series title (postseason)
- **Tony La Russa** (1996–2011); 1,408–1,182 (regular season); 50–42, two World Series titles (postseason)

CAREER BATTING LEADERS

- **Home runs:** Stan Musial, 475
- **RBIs:** Stan Musial, 1,951
- **Runs:** Stan Musial, 1,949
- **Hits:** Stan Musial, 3,630
- **Games played:** Stan Musial, 3,026

CAREER PITCHING LEADERS

- **Wins:** Bob Gibson, 251
- **Saves:** Jason Isringhausen, 217
- **Strikeouts:** Bob Gibson, 3,117
- **Shutouts:** Bob Gibson, 56

GREATEST SEASONS

Expectations were low as the 2011 Cardinals snuck into the playoffs as the NL wild card. But the team got past the Philadelphia Phillies and Milwaukee Brewers to reach the World Series against the Texas Rangers. Texas was one win away and led 7–5 in the bottom of the ninth in Game 6. With two on and two out, third baseman David Freese tripled to tie the game. The Rangers scored twice in the tenth inning, but the Cardinals rallied again to tie it. Finally, Freese, a St. Louis native, led off the bottom of the 11th with a home run to force Game 7. St. Louis won 6–2 and got their 11th World Series title.

Yadier Molina uncoils his swing during a 2021 game.

TEAM HISTORY

The NL added a team in Florida in 1993. However, fans in the northern part of the state had little interest in driving all the way to Miami to see a Marlins game. The Tampa–St. Petersburg area had long been considered a potential market either for expansion or for an existing team to relocate. In 1998, the AL welcomed the Tampa Bay Devil Rays. As an expansion team, they struggled early, averaging 97 losses per season over their first ten years. The team dropped Devil from their nickname in 2008. That same year they reached the playoffs for the first time. In fact, they made it all the way to the World Series, and they soon became regular playoff participants.

Scott Kazmir set a team record (since broken) when he struck out 239 batters in 2007.

GREATEST PLAYERS

- **Rocco Baldelli**, OF (2003–04, 2006–08, 2010)
- **Carl Crawford**, LF (2002–10)
- **Scott Kazmir**, LHP (2004–09)
- **Kevin Kiermaier**, CF (2013–)
- **Evan Longoria**, 3B (2008–17)
- **Carlos Pena**, 1B (2007–10, 2012)

- **David Price**, LHP (2008–14)
- **James Shields**, RHP (2006–12)
- **B. J. Upton**, OF (2004, 2006–12)
- **Ben Zobrist**, 2B-OF (2006–14)

Carl Crawford's potent bat helped the Rays make their first playoff appearance in 2008.

The Rays rush the field after they beat the Baltimore Orioles 5–0 to clinch a 2010 playoff berth.

TEAM STATS AND RECORDS

ALL-TIME RECORD

- **Regular season:** 1,826–1,958
- **Postseason:** 28–32

TOP MANAGERS

- **Joe Maddon** (2006–14); 754–705 (regular season); 13–17 (postseason)
- **Kevin Cash** (2015–); 554–478 (regular season); 15–15 (postseason)

CAREER BATTING LEADERS

- **Home runs:** Evan Longoria, 261
- **RBIs:** Evan Longoria, 892
- **Runs:** Evan Longoria, 780
- **Hits:** Carl Crawford, 1,480
- **Games played:** Evan Longoria, 1,435

CAREER PITCHING LEADERS

- **Wins:** James Shields, 87
- **Saves:** Roberto Hernandez, 101
- **Strikeouts:** James Shields, 1,250
- **Shutouts:** James Shields, 8

JIM MORRIS

Perhaps the most famous rookie in Rays history was Jim Morris. The high school baseball coach from Texas went to an open tryout during the 1999 season. He caught the attention of Rays scouts. Morris made his major league debut a few months later, on September 18, 1999, at age 35. He struck out the only batter he faced in a loss against the Rangers in Texas.

Morris appeared in 21 games for the Rays during the 1999 and 2000 seasons. He struck out 13 batters and had a 4.80 ERA. Morris later wrote a book, *The Oldest Rookie*, which also inspired the 2002 movie *The Rookie*. Actor Dennis Quaid played Morris in the film.

GREATEST SEASONS

In 2020, the COVID-19 pandemic shortened the MLB schedule to just 60 games. The Rays thrived, winning their division by seven games. In the playoffs, they knocked out the Toronto Blue Jays and New York Yankees before going the distance against the Houston Astros in the ALCS. In Game 7, rookie sensation Randy Arozarena bashed a two-run homer in the first inning. The Rays held on to win 4–2. Though they lost to the Los Angeles Dodgers in the World Series, the Rays had given their fans a reason to look back fondly on the 2020 baseball season.

Ji-Man Choi tags out a Dodgers player during Game 6 of the 2020 World Series.

Adolis García advances to second base during a 2021 game.

TEAM HISTORY

The Washington Senators moved to Minnesota in 1961. However, the AL immediately gave the nation's capital a new team. Yet that second version of the Senators was worse than the first. They averaged 100 losses over their first five seasons. They routinely finished at the bottom of the league standings. In 1972, owner Bob Short moved the team to the Dallas–Fort Worth area. He renamed them the Texas Rangers. But the losing continued. The Rangers didn't reach the playoffs until 1996 and didn't win their first AL pennant until 2010.

GREATEST PLAYERS

- **Elvis Andrus**, SS (2009–20)
- **Buddy Bell**, 3B (1979–85, 1989)
- **Adrián Beltré**, 3B (2011–18)
- **Juan González**, OF (1989–99, 2002–03)
- **Charlie Hough**, RHP (1980–90)
- **Rafael Palmeiro**, 1B (1989–93, 1999–2003)
- **Iván Rodríguez**, C (1991–2002, 2009)
- **Kenny Rogers**, LHP (1989–95, 2000–02, 2004–05)
- **Jim Sundberg**, C (1974–83, 1988–89)
- **Michael Young**, INF (2000–12)

Alex Rodriguez became the youngest player to hit 300 home runs when he reached the milestone on April 2, 2003.

TEAM STATS AND RECORDS

ALL-TIME RECORD

- **Regular season:** 4,582–5,052
- **Postseason:** 21–31

TOP MANAGERS

- **Bobby Valentine** (1985–92); 581–605 (regular season)
- **Ron Washington** (2007–14); 664–611 (regular season); 18–16 (postseason)

CAREER BATTING LEADERS

- **Home runs:** Juan González, 372
- **RBIs:** Juan González, 1,180
- **Runs:** Michael Young, 1,085
- **Hits:** Michael Young, 2,230
- **Games played:** Michael Young, 1,823

CAREER PITCHING LEADERS

- **Wins:** Charlie Hough, 139
- **Saves:** John Wetteland, 150
- **Strikeouts:** Charlie Hough, 1,452
- **Shutouts:** Fergie Jenkins, 17

Fergie Jenkins had a franchise-record 25 wins in 1974. He pitched for the Rangers in 1974 and 1975 and again from 1978 to 1981.

NOLAN RYAN AND THE RANGERS

Texas native Nolan Ryan pitched for the Rangers from 1989 to 1993. He became the first player to enter the Baseball Hall of Fame wearing a Rangers cap. He played an MLB-record 27 seasons and finished with a record 5,714 career strikeouts. While with the Rangers, the right-hander notched his 5,000th career strikeout in 1989, earned his 300th victory in 1990, and tossed two no-hitters. He is the oldest pitcher to throw a no-hitter. Nicknamed "Ryan Express," his fastball topped out around 100 miles per hour (161 kmh).

Ryan returned as the Rangers' president in 2008. He helped put together the team that won the 2010 pennant. He was also part of a group that bought the team in 2010 and served as the Rangers CEO through the 2013 season.

GREATEST SEASONS

The Rangers entered the 2010 season having never played in the World Series. But coming off a strong 2009 season, they appeared to be on the brink of something special. After taking over first place in the AL West in June, the Rangers traded for ace lefty Cliff Lee. He proved to be well worth the investment. Lee helped Texas win the division. Then he won his first three postseason starts, averaging eight innings in each, as the Rangers defeated Tampa Bay and the Yankees. Although they fell to the San Francisco Giants in the World Series, 2010 was a year to remember for the Rangers.

Pitcher Cliff Lee helped the Rangers reach the 2010 World Series.

TEAM HISTORY

The NL went to Canada in 1969 with the birth of the Montreal Expos. In 1977, it was the AL's turn to expand north of the border. It added the Toronto Blue Jays to the league. The Jays played their games at Exhibition Stadium, which was a football field that had to be adjusted for baseball. Spring and fall dates were often cold and windy in Toronto. So in 1989 the city built a retractable-roof stadium. Perhaps coincidentally, the Blue Jays won the AL East four times in the next five seasons. In two of those years, they won the World Series. Through 2021, that was still the only time a Canadian team had won MLB's biggest prize.

Joe Carter watches as his hit sails over the outfield fence for the game-winning home run in the 1993 World Series.

Blue Jays shortstop Tony Fernández leaps to avoid a sliding Oakland A's runner during the 1989 playoffs.

GREATEST PLAYERS

- **Roberto Alomar**, 2B (1991–95)
- **Jesse Barfield**, RF (1981–89)
- **José Bautista**, RF (2008–17)
- **Joe Carter**, OF (1991–97)
- **Carlos Delgado**, 1B (1993–2004)
- **Tony Fernández**, SS (1983–90, 1993, 1998–99, 2001)

- **Roy Halladay**, RHP (1998–2009)
- **John Olerud**, 1B (1989–96)
- **Dave Stieb**, RHP (1979–92, 1998)
- **Vernon Wells**, CF (1999–2010)

Vladimir Guerrero Jr. slides home during a 2021 game.

TEAM STATS AND RECORDS

ALL-TIME RECORD

- **Regular season:** 3,506–3,557
- **Postseason:** 31–32, two World Series titles

TOP MANAGERS

- **Cito Gaston** (1989–97, 2008–10); 894–837 (regular season); 18–16, two World Series titles (postseason)
- **John Gibbons** (2004–08, 2013–18); 793–789 (regular season); 10–10 (postseason)

CAREER BATTING LEADERS

- **Home runs:** Carlos Delgado, 336
- **RBIs:** Carlos Delgado, 1,058
- **Runs:** Carlos Delgado, 889
- **Hits:** Tony Fernández, 1,583
- **Games played:** Tony Fernández, 1,450

CAREER PITCHING LEADERS

- **Wins:** Dave Stieb, 175
- **Saves:** Tom Henke, 217
- **Strikeouts:** Dave Stieb, 1,658
- **Shutouts:** Dave Stieb, 30

GREATEST SEASONS

The Blue Jays won back-to-back World Series in the early 1990s, defeating the Atlanta Braves in six games in 1992 and doing the same to the Philadelphia Phillies in 1993. Both times, the Jays got a big hit from one of their big stars to clinch the final game. Against the Braves, future Hall of Famer Dave Winfield hit a two-out, two-run double in the 11th inning to put Toronto on top. And a year later, trailing 6–5 with one out in the ninth inning, right fielder Joe Carter blasted a three-run homer to end it. It was the first walk-off homer to clinch the World Series since the Pirates' Bill Mazeroski did it in 1960.

The Blue Jays brought in veteran designated hitter Paul Molitor for the 1993 season. He became the 1993 World Series MVP.

COVID-19 AND THE BLUE JAYS

The COVID-19 pandemic caused a major disruption to all MLB teams, but none more than the Blue Jays. The Canadian government, citing the need to limit the spread the virus, placed restrictions on international travel. That meant Toronto's opponents would have a hard time crossing the border to play them. As a result, the Blue Jays decided to play their home games in Buffalo, New York, at the stadium of their Triple-A team. When the 2021 season began, the restrictions had not been lifted, and the ballpark in Buffalo was getting renovated. So the Blue Jays started the season playing home games at their spring training facility in Dunedin, Florida.

TEAM HISTORY

NL expansion brought MLB to Canada for the first time in 1969 with the founding of the Montreal Expos. The team won a single division title, and the Expos were in first place when a labor dispute cut short the 1994 season. That disappointment

Liván Hernández helped the Nationals start quickly in 2005, which was the franchise's first year in Washington.

MONTREAL'S BASEBALL HISTORY

Montreal was no stranger to baseball before the Expos came to town. The city had been a host to minor league teams as far back as the 1890s. Many of them were called the Royals. Before he debuted with the Brooklyn Dodgers in 1947, Jackie Robinson spent the 1946 season with the Triple-A Montreal Royals.

damaged an already fragile relationship with the Montreal fans. Unable to secure funding for a new stadium, the Expos' owners sold the team. Soon it moved to Washington, DC, and became the Nationals. The nation's capital had been without a team since the AL Senators moved to Texas in 1972.

GREATEST PLAYERS

- **Gary Carter**, C (1974–84, 1992)
- **Andre Dawson**, OF (1976–86)
- **Bryce Harper**, RF (2012–18)
- **Tim Raines**, OF (1979–90)
- **Anthony Rendon**, 3B (2013–19)
- **Steve Rogers**, RHP (1973–85)
- **Max Scherzer**, RHP (2015–21)
- **Juan Soto**, OF (2018–)
- **Stephen Strasburg**, RHP (2010–)
- **Ryan Zimmerman**, 3B-1B (2005–19, 2021)

Ryan Zimmerman's longevity with the team has earned him the nickname "Mr. National."

TEAM STATS AND RECORDS

ALL-TIME RECORD

- **Regular season:** 4,068–4,280
- **Postseason:** 24–22, one World Series title

TOP MANAGERS

- **Felipe Alou** (1992–2001); 691–717 (regular season)
- **Buck Rodgers** (1985–91); 520–499 (regular season)

CAREER BATTING LEADERS

- **Home runs:** Ryan Zimmerman, 284
- **RBIs:** Ryan Zimmerman, 1,061
- **Runs:** Ryan Zimmerman, 963
- **Hits:** Ryan Zimmerman, 1,846
- **Games played:** Ryan Zimmerman, 1,799

CAREER PITCHING LEADERS

- **Wins:** Steve Rogers, 158
- **Saves:** Jeff Reardon, 152
- **Strikeouts:** Stephen Strasburg, 1,718
- **Shutouts:** Steve Rogers, 37

GREATEST SEASONS

The Montreal Expos were loaded with young talent in the early 1990s. The pieces were in place for a run to their first World Series in 1994. The outfield included All-Stars Moises Alou (.339 batting average), Marquis Grissom (36 stolen bases), and Larry Walker (.322, 44 doubles). A deep starting rotation was backed by a dominant bullpen. On August 10, Pedro Martinez helped shut out the Pittsburgh Pirates to give Montreal its 20th win in its previous 22 games. But the season ended the next day when the players went on strike. The Expos had the best record in baseball at 74–40, but they never got to play for the title.

In 2019, the Washington Nationals qualified for the NL playoffs as a wild card. A tenth-inning grand slam by Howie Kendrick lifted them over the Los Angeles Dodgers in the final game of the NLDS. That led to a sweep of the St. Louis Cardinals in the NLCS, setting up a thrilling World Series against the Houston Astros. Trailing three games to two, the Nationals won the final two games in Houston to give them their first World Series championship.

The Nationals swarm the field after clinching the World Series in 2019.

HANK AARON RF

Milwaukee Braves (1954–65), Atlanta Braves (1966–74), Milwaukee Brewers (1975–76); Negro Leagues: Indianapolis Clowns (1952)

A feared power hitter for more than two decades, Hank Aaron was one of the last players with Negro Leagues experience to reach the major leagues.

He proved to be one of the most remarkably consistent hitters in MLB history. He holds MLB career records for RBIs, total bases, and All-Star Game appearances. His most famous moment came on April 8, 1974, when he homered off the Dodgers' Al Downing at Atlanta-Fulton County Stadium. That gave him 715 career homers, breaking Babe Ruth's record.

Hank Aaron

Games: 3,298   **RBIs:** 2,297
Hits: 3,771   **AVG:** .305
HRs: 755
Awards: NL MVP (1957), 25 All-Star Games, three Gold Gloves

JOHNNY BENCH C-3B

Cincinnati Reds (1967–83)

Johnny Bench was a key cog of Cincinnati's "Big Red Machine" that dominated the NL in the 1970s. He pioneered a one-handed style of catching, keeping his bare hand tucked behind his back. Bench played an average of 145 games a year from 1968 through 1979. He led the majors in both home runs and RBIs in 1970 and 1972. He also hit .533 with two homers in a four-game sweep of the New York Yankees in the 1976 World Series.

Games: 2,158   **RBIs:** 1,376
Hits: 2,048   **AVG:** .267
HRs: 389
Awards: NL Rookie of the Year (1968), NL MVP (1970, 1972), World Series MVP (1976), 14 All-Star Games, ten Gold Gloves

Johnny Bench

YOGI BERRA C-OF

New York Yankees (1946–63), New York Mets (1965)

One of the game's all-time great characters, Yogi Berra is credited with numerous offbeat quotes and expressions about baseball and life. Whether he actually said, "It ain't over until it's over" or "It's like *déjà vu* all over again" is a topic of dispute. But his contributions to the Yankee dynasty are etched in stone. Berra won ten World Series rings and went on to manage pennant-winning teams for both the Yankees and the Mets.

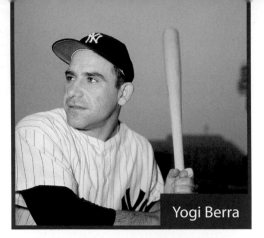

Yogi Berra

Games: 2,120   **RBIs:** 1,430
Hits: 2,150   **AVG:** .285
HRs: 358
Awards: AL MVP (1951, 1954, 1955), 18 All-Star Games

BARRY BONDS LF

Pittsburgh Pirates (1986–92), San Francisco Giants (1993–2007)

Barry Bonds hit more home runs than any other player in MLB history. Though the latter half of his career was clouded by accusations that he used illegal, performance-enhancing drugs, his skills were unquestioned. His total of seven MVP awards is four more than any other player. In 1996, Bonds became just the second player ever with at least 40 home runs and 40 stolen bases in a season. And his 73 home runs in 2001 is a record many believe will never be broken.

Games: 2,986   **RBIs:** 1,996
Hits: 2,935   **AVG:** .298
HRs: 762
Awards: NL MVP (1990, 1992–93, 2001–04), 14 All-Star Games, eight Gold Gloves, 12 Silver Sluggers

Barry Bonds

ROD CAREW 2B-1B

Minnesota Twins (1967–78), California Angels (1979–85)

Rod Carew was a singles and doubles machine throughout the 1970s. His seven AL batting titles are second only to the legendary Ty Cobb, and the award for the AL batting title is now named for Carew. He won six of his titles in a seven-year span beginning in 1972, with his average topping out at .388 in 1977. Carew was also an excellent base runner who stole home seven times in 1969, one shy of the MLB record.

Rod Carew

Games: 2,469 **RBIs:** 1,015
Hits: 3,053 **AVG:** .328
HRs: 92
Awards: AL Rookie of the Year (1967), AL MVP (1977), 18 All-Star Games

STEVE CARLTON LHP

St. Louis Cardinals (1965–71), Philadelphia Phillies (1972–86), San Francisco Giants (1986), Chicago White Sox (1986), Cleveland Indians (1987), Minnesota Twins (1987–88)

Steve Carlton won the 1972 NL pitching Triple Crown when he went 27–10 with 310 strikeouts and a 1.97 ERA. What made that even more remarkable was that his Philadelphia Phillies team won just 59 games that year. Carlton went on to lead the NL in victories three more times and in strikeouts four times.

Steve Carlton

Games: 741
Innings Pitched: 5,217.2
W-L: 329–244
ERA: 3.22
Strikeouts: 4,136
Awards: NL Cy Young (1972, 1977, 1980, 1982), ten All-Star Games

ROGER CLEMENS RHP

Boston Red Sox (1984–96), Toronto Blue Jays (1997–98), New York Yankees (1999–2003, 2007), Houston Astros (2004–06)

Roger Clemens was one of baseball's most intimidating pitchers for two decades. His seven Cy Young Awards are a record. However, he was accused of using illegal, performance-enhancing drugs. Because of this, Hall of Fame voters decided to not immediately add Clemens when he became eligible.

Games: 709
Innings Pitched: 4,916.2
W-L: 354–184
ERA: 3.12
Strikeouts: 4,672
Awards: AL Cy Young (1986–87, 1991, 1997–98, 2001), NL Cy Young (2004), AL MVP (1986), 11 All-Star Games

Roger Clemens

ROBERTO CLEMENTE RF

Pittsburgh Pirates (1955–72)

Roberto Clemente is best remembered for his rifle arm that he used to put fear in the hearts of opposing base runners. But his offensive game was strong too. He won four NL batting titles, hitting a career-high .357 when he won his fourth in 1967. In the 1971 postseason he hit .383 to lead the Pittsburgh Pirates to a World Series victory. He recorded his 3,000th career hit in the 1972 season.

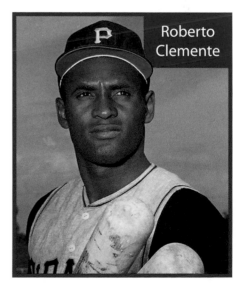
Roberto Clemente

Games: 2,433   **RBIs:** 1,305
Hits: 3,000   **AVG:** .317
HRs: 240
Awards: NL MVP (1966), World Series MVP (1971), 15 All-Star Games, 12 Gold Gloves

TY COBB OF

Detroit Tigers (1905–26), Philadelphia Athletics (1927–28)

Ty Cobb was one of the finest hitters ever to play baseball. His .366 career batting average is the best of all time, and his 12 league batting titles is a mark likely never to be matched. He retired with 897 career stolen bases, an MLB record that stood until 1977.

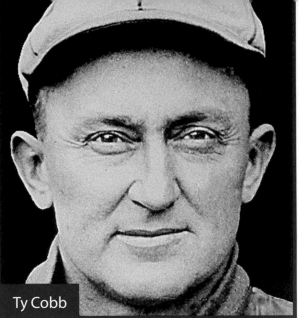

Ty Cobb

Games: 3,034   **RBIs:** 1,944
Hits: 4,189   **AVG:** .366
HRs: 117
Awards: AL MVP (1911)

DENNIS ECKERSLEY RHP

Cleveland Indians (1975–77), Boston Red Sox (1978–84, 1998), Chicago Cubs (1984–86), Oakland Athletics (1987–95), St. Louis Cardinals (1996–97)

Dennis Eckersley was a two-time All-Star as a starting pitcher. He threw a no-hitter for Cleveland in 1977 and won 20 games for the Red Sox in 1978. But Eckersley reinvented himself as a reliever when he joined the Oakland Athletics in 1987. He spent the next decade as one of the league's most feared closers. Eckersley twice led the majors in saves, posting a career-high 51 in 1992.

Games: 1,071
Innings Pitched: 3,285.2
W-L: 197–171
Saves: 390
ERA: 3.50
Strikeouts: 2,401
Awards: AL Cy Young (1992), AL MVP (1992), ALCS MVP (1988), six All-Star Games

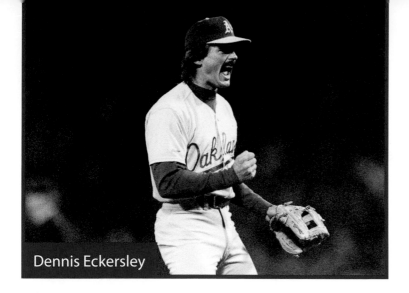

Dennis Eckersley

BOB FELLER RHP

Cleveland Indians (1936–41, 1945–56)

Bob Feller made his debut at age 17. He soon became one of the AL's most dominating pitchers. He used an overpowering fastball to lead the majors in strikeouts for four straight seasons, beginning in 1938. Feller also won 93 games over those four years. He missed the next three seasons while serving in World War II, but he returned to form quickly, winning 26 games and striking out a career-best 348 hitters in 1946.

Bob Feller

Games: 570
Innings Pitched: 3,827
W-L: 266–162
ERA: 3.25
Strikeouts: 2,581
Awards: Eight All-Star Games

WHITEY FORD LHP

New York Yankees (1950, 1953–67)

Whitey Ford was an outstanding all-around pitcher. He appeared in 11 World Series, helping the New York Yankees win six of them. Ford set World Series records with 22 games started, ten victories, 94 strikeouts, and almost 34 consecutive scoreless innings from 1960 to 1962.

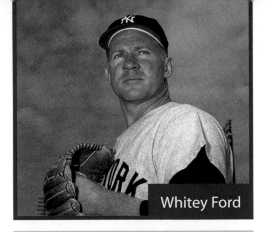
Whitey Ford

Games: 498
Innings Pitched: 3,170.1
W-L: 236–106
ERA: 2.75
Strikeouts: 1,956
Awards: AL Cy Young (1961), World Series MVP (1961), ten All-Star Games

JIMMIE FOXX 1B

Philadelphia Athletics (1925–35), Boston Red Sox (1936–42), Chicago Cubs (1942, 1944), Philadelphia Phillies (1945)

Jimmie Foxx was a stocky slugger who led the AL in home runs four times, including a career-best 58 in 1932. He was also just the second player to hit 500 career home runs. Foxx was an RBI machine, driving in at least 100 runs in 13 straight seasons.

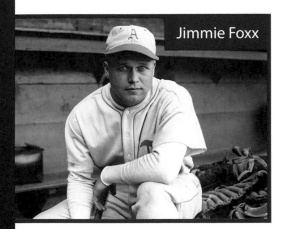
Jimmie Foxx

Games: 2,317 **RBIs:** 1,922
Hits: 2,646   **AVG:** .325
HRs: 534
Awards: AL MVP (1932–33, 1938), nine All-Star Games

Lou Gehrig

LOU GEHRIG 1B
New York Yankees (1923–39)

Lou Gehrig put up astounding numbers and led the New York Yankees to victory after victory. Gehrig set a record by playing in 2,130 consecutive games. Along the way, he hit 23 career grand slams, drove in at least 100 runs in 13 straight seasons, and won the 1934 Triple Crown when he hit .363 with 49 homers and 166 RBIs.

Games: 2,164　**RBIs:** 1,995
Hits: 2,721　**AVG:** .340
HRs: 493
Awards: AL MVP (1927, 1936), seven All-Star Games

BOB GIBSON RHP

St. Louis Cardinals (1959–75)

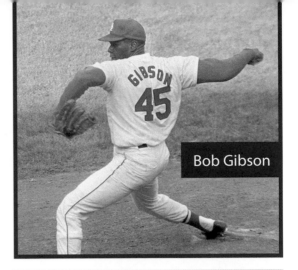

Bob Gibson

One of the most intimidating pitchers of all time, Bob Gibson helped lead the St. Louis Cardinals to World Series titles in 1964 and 1967. But it was his performance in 1968 that turned baseball on its head. Gibson set a modern-era record with a 1.12 ERA. He also threw 28 complete games, including 13 shutouts. And in Game 1 of the World Series, he struck out 17 players, a record that remains untouched.

Games: 528
Innings Pitched: 3,884.1
W-L: 251–174
ERA: 2.91
Strikeouts: 3,117
Awards: NL Cy Young (1968, 1970), NL MVP (1968), World Series MVP (1964, 1967), nine All-Star Games, nine Gold Gloves

JOSH GIBSON C

Negro Leagues: Homestead Grays (1930–31, 1937–40, 1942–46), Pittsburgh Crawfords (1932–36)

Josh Gibson

Josh Gibson spent his entire career in the Negro Leagues. Because MLB was not integrated during his playing days, fans will never know how Gibson would've fared against the well-known major league pitchers of the era. But tales of his legendary home runs suggest he'd have been among the best hitters the game has ever seen. Statistical records from the Negro League days are incomplete, but Gibson's plaque at the Baseball Hall of Fame says that he hit "almost 800 home runs in league and independent baseball during his 17-year career."

Ken Griffey Jr.

KEN GRIFFEY JR. OF

Seattle Mariners (1989–99, 2009–10), Cincinnati Reds (2000–08), Chicago White Sox (2008)

Ken Griffey Jr.'s sweet swing, thrilling catches in center field, and smile helped remind fans the game was supposed to be fun. He was the son of longtime Cincinnati Reds outfielder Ken Sr. The two actually played together in Seattle for parts of two seasons. Junior went on to outpace his father—and virtually every other player—with his mammoth home runs and fence-busting catches to rob opposing batters of extra-base hits.

Games: 2,671   **RBIs:** 1,836
Hits: 2,781   **AVG:** .284
HRs: 630
Awards: AL MVP (1997), 13 All-Star Games, ten Gold Gloves, seven Silver Sluggers

TONY GWYNN RF

San Diego Padres (1982–2001)

Tony Gwynn

Tony Gwynn earned eight NL batting titles in his career. He never posted a batting average below .309 for a full season. He topped out at .394 in 1994, missing out on a shot at .400 when a players' strike cut the season short in mid-August. In a five-season stretch that began in 1993, Gwynn hit an amazing .368 and struck out just 98 times in nearly 2,500 at bats. The award for the NL batting title is now named for Gwynn.

Games: 2,440 **RBIs:** 1,138
Hits: 3,141 **AVG:** .338
HRs: 135
Awards: 15 All-Star Games, five Gold Gloves, seven Silver Sluggers

RICKEY HENDERSON OF

Oakland Athletics (1979–84, 1989–93, 1994–95, 1998), New York Yankees (1985–89), Toronto Blue Jays, (1993), San Diego Padres (1996–97, 2001), Anaheim Angels (1997), New York Mets (1999–2000), Seattle Mariners (2000), Boston Red Sox (2002), Los Angeles Dodgers (2003)

Rickey Henderson is regarded as the greatest leadoff hitter in MLB history. He hit 81 leadoff homers, but he could just as easily draw a walk that he often turned into a two bases with his remarkable speed. Henderson holds the MLB record with 130 stolen bases in a season and 1,406 career steals.

Games: 3,081 **RBIs:** 1,115
Hits: 3,055 **AVG:** .279
HRs: 297
Awards: AL MVP (1990), ALCS MVP (1989), ten All-Star Games, one Gold Glove, three Silver Sluggers

ROGERS HORNSBY 2B

St. Louis Cardinals (1915–26, 1933), New York Giants (1927), Boston Braves (1928), Chicago Cubs (1929–32), St. Louis Browns (1933–37)

Rogers Hornsby's career batting average is second in MLB history. He also won the NL Triple Crown in 1922 when he hit .401 with 42 homers and 152 RBIs. He did the trick again three years later, leading both leagues with a .403 batting average, 39 homers, and 143 RBIs.

Games: 2,259   **RBIs:** 1,584
Hits: 2,930   **AVG:** .358
HRs: 301
Awards: NL MVP (1925, 1929)

Rogers Hornsby

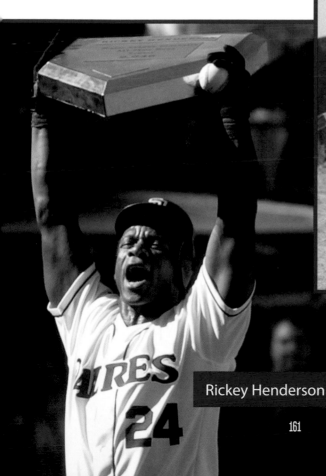

Rickey Henderson

DEREK JETER SS

New York Yankees (1995–2014)

The longtime captain of the New York Yankees joined the squad just as it began its five-year run as the best team in the majors. Derek

Derek Jeter

Jeter's steady defense, timely hits, and calm leadership helped the Yankees win four World Series between 1996 and 2000. He stuck around for their 2009 title as well, and three years later, at age 38, he led the majors with 216 hits.

Games: 2,747
Hits: 3,465
HRs: 260
RBIs: 1,311
AVG: .310
Awards: AL Rookie of the Year (1996), World Series MVP (2000), 14 All-Star Games, five Gold Gloves, five Silver Sluggers

RANDY JOHNSON LHP

Montreal Expos (1988–89), Seattle Mariners (1989–98), Houston Astros (1998), Arizona Diamondbacks (1999–2004, 2007–08), New York Yankees (2005–06), San Francisco Giants (2009)

Randy Johnson was known as the "Big Unit." The 6-foot-10 lefty had an overpowering fastball. He's the only pitcher to win four straight Cy Young Awards with the same team. Johnson also led the league in strikeouts nine times. He started at least 30 games 13 times in a 17-year span. In Game 7 of the 2001 World Series, Johnson came out of the bullpen one day after pitching seven innings and retired four straight batters to help the Arizona Diamondbacks defeat the New York Yankees.

Randy Johnson

Games: 618
Innings Pitched: 4,135.1
W-L: 303–166
ERA: 3.29
Strikeouts: 4,875
Awards: AL Cy Young (1995), NL Cy Young (1999–2002), World Series MVP (2001), ten All-Star Games

WALTER JOHNSON RHP

Washington Senators (1907–27)

Walter Johnson rode his remarkable fastball to the second-most victories of any pitcher in MLB history. He led the league in victories six times and claimed 12 strikeout crowns. He also posted the league's lowest ERA five times, winning the AL pitching Triple Crown in 1913, 1918, and 1924. He retired as the league's all-time strikeout king, and his 110 career shutouts are among baseball's untouchable records.

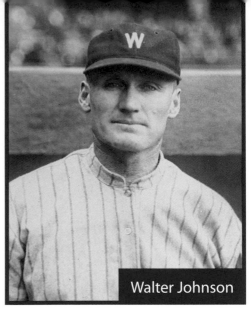

Walter Johnson

Games: 802
Innings Pitched: 5,914.1
W-L: 417–279
ERA: 2.17
Strikeouts: 3,509
Awards: AL MVP (1913, 1924)

CLAYTON KERSHAW LHP

Los Angeles Dodgers (2008–)

The latest in a long line of dominant Dodgers pitchers, Clayton Kershaw debuted with the team at age 20. Three years later he won the NL pitching Triple Crown with 21 wins, 248 strikeouts, and a 2.28 ERA. That was the first of four straight ERA titles, capped by a remarkable 2014 season in which he went 21–3 with a 1.77 ERA.

Games: 379
Innings Pitched: 2,454.2
W-L: 185–84
ERA: 2.49
Strikeouts: 2,670
Awards: NL Cy Young (2011, 2013–14), NL MVP (2014), eight All-Star Games, one Gold Glove

Clayton Kershaw

SANDY KOUFAX LHP

Brooklyn Dodgers (1955–57), Los Angeles Dodgers (1958–66)

Sandy Koufax has one of the most dominant stretches of any pitcher in MLB history. Starting in 1961, Koufax led the NL in strikeouts four times and in ERA five times over the next six years. He also won four of his five World Series starts as the Dodgers took the title in 1963 and 1965.

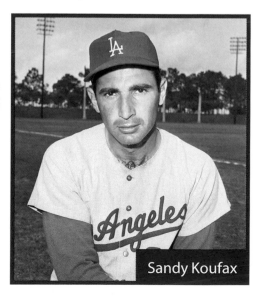

Sandy Koufax

Games: 397
Innings Pitched: 2,324.1
W–L: 165–87
ERA: 2.76
Strikeouts: 2,396
Awards: Cy Young (1963, 1965–66), NL MVP (1963), World Series MVP (1963, 1965), seven All-Star Games

GREG MADDUX RHP

Chicago Cubs (1986–92, 2004–06), Atlanta Braves (1993–2003), Los Angeles Dodgers (2006, 2008), San Diego Padres (2007–08)

Greg Maddux

The greatest control pitcher of his generation, Greg Maddux made a living on the corners of the plate. He proved that a pitcher doesn't need to be overpowering to be dominant. He claimed four NL ERA titles and won at least 13 games in 19 straight seasons. He's also one of

Games: 744
Innings Pitched: 5,008.1
W-L: 355–227
ERA: 3.16
Strikeouts: 3,371
Awards: NL Cy Young (1992–95), eight All-Star Games, 18 Gold Gloves

only two pitchers to win four straight Cy Young Awards, and he's the only one to win it in consecutive seasons with two different teams.

MICKEY MANTLE OF

New York Yankees (1951–68)

The switch-hitting center fielder Mickey Mantle was the biggest star of the great New York Yankees teams of the 1950s and early 1960s. A knee injury suffered early in his career kept him from reaching his full potential. But he still managed to win the AL Triple Crown in 1956 and led the AL in home runs four times.

Games: 2,401   **RBIs:** 1,509
Hits: 2,415   **AVG:** .298
HRs: 536
Awards: AL MVP (1956–57, 1962), 20 All-Star Games, one Gold Glove

Mickey Mantle

PEDRO MARTÍNEZ RHP

Los Angeles Dodgers (1992–93), Montreal Expos (1994–97), Boston Red Sox (1998–2004), New York Mets (2005–08), Philadelphia Phillies (2009)

Pedro Martínez is the only pitcher with more than 3,000 career strikeouts in fewer than 3,000 career innings. The five-time league ERA champ went an eye-popping 23–4 with a 2.07 ERA and 313 strikeouts in 1999 to win the AL pitching Triple Crown. Martínez will forever be a beloved figure in Boston, where he helped the Red Sox break their World Series drought in 2004.

Pedro Martínez

Games: 476
Innings Pitched: 2,827.1
W-L: 219–100
ERA: 2.93
Strikeouts: 3,154
Awards: NL Cy Young (1997), AL Cy Young (1999–2000), eight All-Star Games

WILLIE MAYS CF

Birmingham Black Barons (1948), New York Giants (1951–52, 1954–57), San Francisco Giants (1958–72), New York Mets (1972–73)

Willie Mays has been called the greatest ever to play the game, and it's hard to say there was anyone clearly better. Mays retired with more home runs than any right-handed hitter. He also led the NL in stolen bases four times and drove in at least 100 runs in a season ten times.

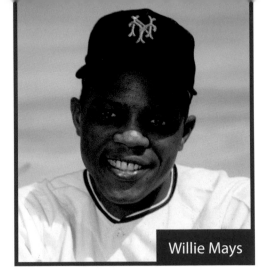

Willie Mays

Games: 3,005   **RBIs:** 1,909
Hits: 3,293   **AVG:** .301
HRs: 660
Awards: NL MVP (1954, 1965), 24 All-Star Games, 12 Gold Gloves

Joe Morgan

JOE MORGAN 2B

*Houston Colt .45s (1963–64),
Houston Astros (1965–71, 1980),
Cincinnati Reds (1972–79), San
Francisco Giants (1981–82),
Philadelphia Phillies (1983),
Oakland Athletics (1984)*

Games: 2,649   **RBIs:** 1,133
Hits: 2,517   **AVG:** .271
HRs: 268
Awards: NL MVP (1975–76),
ten All-Star Games, five Gold
Gloves, one Silver Slugger

Joe Morgan led the NL in on-base percentage four times. He also
hit more than 20 home runs four times. But he made his greatest
impact on the bases. Between 1969 and 1977, he stole at least 40
bases every season, including a career-high 67 steals in 1973 that he
matched two years later.

STAN MUSIAL OF-1B

St. Louis Cardinals (1941–44, 1946–63)

Stan Musial won seven batting
titles and was remarkably
consistent in the power game too.
He hit at least ten home runs in
every season but his first, when he
played just 12 games. From 1946
to 1957, he averaged 110 RBIs
per season.

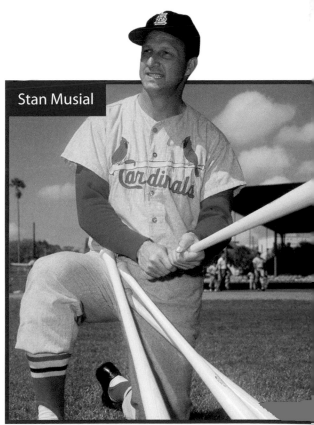

Stan Musial

Games: 3,026
Hits: 3,630
HRs: 475
RBIs: 1,951
AVG: .331
Awards: NL MVP (1943, 1946,
1948), 24 All-Star Games

Satchel Paige

SATCHEL PAIGE RHP

Cleveland Indians (1948–49), St. Louis Browns (1951–53), Kansas City Athletics (1965); also at least 11 Negro Leagues teams, most notably the Pittsburgh Crawfords (1932–34, 1936) and Kansas City Monarchs (1935, 1939–47)

Satchel Paige had a long career in the Negro Leagues. He established himself as one of the game's best pitchers. Page joined the Cleveland Indians at age 41, one year after Jackie Robinson broke the color barrier. Paige went 6–1 with a 2.48 ERA and helped Cleveland win the World Series in his "rookie" season. In his prime, he relied on a deadly fastball and pinpoint control to dominate hitters.

Games: 391
Innings Pitched: 1,695
W-L: 118–80
ERA: 2.70
Strikeouts: 1,438
Awards: Two MLB All-Star Games, eight Negro League All-Star Games

JIM PALMER RHP

Baltimore Orioles (1965–67, 1969–84)

Jim Palmer was one of the game's top pitchers. He won 20 games in eight different seasons, and his 186 victories in the 1970s were the most of anyone in the decade.

Games: 558
Innings Pitched: 3,948
W-L: 268–152
ERA: 2.86
Strikeouts: 2,212
Awards: AL Cy Young (1973, 1975–76), six All-Star Games, four Gold Gloves

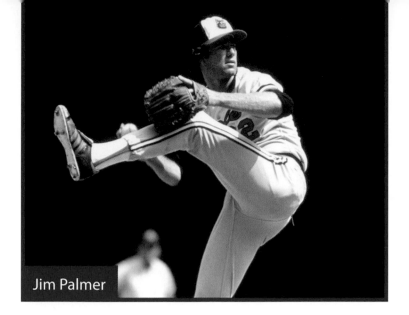

Jim Palmer

ALBERT PUJOLS 1B-3B-OF-DH

St. Louis Cardinals (2001–11), Los Angeles Angels (2012–21), Los Angeles Dodgers (2021–)

One of the game's most feared sluggers, Albert Pujols was a complete hitter who led MLB with a .359 batting average in 2003 when he was just 23 years old. He went on to hit at least 40 homers in a season seven times and drove in at least 100 runs in each of his first ten MLB seasons. Pujols helped carry the St. Louis Cardinals to two World Series titles before leaving for Los Angeles.

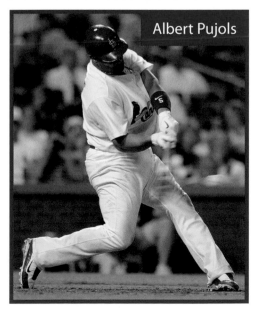

Albert Pujols

Games: 2,971 **RBIs:** 2,150
Hits: 3,301 **AVG:** .297
HRs: 679
Awards: NL Rookie of the Year (2001), NL MVP (2005, 2008–09), NLCS MVP (2004), ten All-Star Games, two Gold Gloves, six Silver Sluggers

CAL RIPKEN JR. SS-3B

Baltimore Orioles (1981–2001)

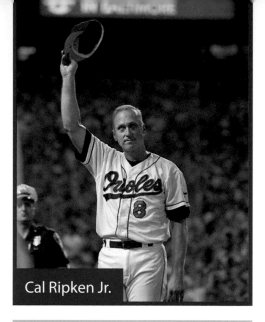

Cal Ripken Jr.

Cal Ripken Jr. broke Lou Gehrig's consecutive games record in 1995. He eventually ended his streak at 2,632, more than 500 games longer than Gehrig's. But he was more than just a durable player. Ripken was one of the game's first modern shortstops. He was tall and rangy with great power at the plate. He led the Orioles to a World Series title in just his second full season in the majors. He finished his career by hitting a home run in his final All-Star Game, earning the game's MVP honors in 2001.

Games: 3,001 **RBIs:** 1,695
Hits: 3,184 **AVG:** .276
HRs: 431
Awards: AL Rookie of the Year (1982), AL MVP (1983, 1991), 19 All-Star Games, two Gold Gloves, eight Silver Sluggers

MARIANO RIVERA RHP

New York Yankees (1995–2013)

Games: 1,115
Innings Pitched: 1,283.2
W-L: 82–60
Saves: 652
ERA: 2.21
Strikeouts: 1,173
Awards: World Series MVP (1999), ALCS MVP (2003), 13 All-Star Games

It's hard to dominate on the mound with one pitch, but Mariano Rivera was able to use his patented cutter to post the most saves in MLB history. Rivera's pitches moved so much that batters had a difficult time hitting them on the barrel, resulting in numerous broken bats and weak ground balls or pop-ups. Rivera was especially deadly in the postseason, where his 0.70 ERA and 42 saves are MLB career records.

Mariano Rivera

FRANK ROBINSON OF-1B

Cincinnati Reds (1956–65), Baltimore Orioles (1966–71), Los Angeles Dodgers (1972), California Angels (1973–74), Cleveland Indians (1974–76)

Games: 2,808 **RBIs:** 1,812
Hits: 2,943 **AVG:** .294
HRs: 586
Awards: NL Rookie of the Year (1956), NL MVP (1961), AL MVP (1966), World Series MVP (1966), 14 All-Star Games, one Gold Glove

Power-hitting Frank Robinson is the only player to win an MVP Award in both the NL and AL. He led his teams to the World Series in both of his MVP seasons, and he helped the Baltimore Orioles win their first championship in 1966. Robinson won the AL Triple Crown that season, and he retired with the third-most home runs of any right-handed hitter. He also became the first Black manager in MLB history.

Frank Robinson

Jackie Robinson

JACKIE ROBINSON 2B-1B-3B-OF

Brooklyn Dodgers (1947–56); Negro Leagues: Kansas City Monarchs (1945)

Jackie Robinson has been called one of the most important figures of the 1900s, and not just in sports. The Brooklyn Dodgers chose him to integrate MLB in 1947 because they felt he had the temperament to handle the racial abuse he was sure to face. But he also had unique skills on the diamond. A versatile fielder and dynamic base runner, Robinson helped lead the Dodgers to six NL pennants. His No. 42 is the only number retired throughout MLB.

Games: 1,416   **RBIs:** 761
Hits: 1,563   **AVG:** .313
HRs: 141
Awards: NL Rookie of the Year (1947), NL MVP (1949), seven All-Star Games

PETE ROSE OF-1B-3B-2B

Cincinnati Reds (1963–78, 1984–86), Philadelphia Phillies (1979–83), Montreal Expos (1984)

Pete Rose has his name all over the record books. He holds MLB records for games played, at bats, and hits. Rose's fiery brand of play earned him the admiration of baseball fans around the league, but especially in his native Cincinnati, where he helped lead the Reds to a pair of World Series titles. He left for Philadelphia as a free agent, and in his second year with the Phillies, he helped deliver their first title. He was later banned from baseball for gambling on games when he was a manager.

Games: 3,562   **RBIs:** 1,314
Hits: 4,256   **AVG:** .303
HRs: 160
Awards: NL Rookie of the Year (1963), NL MVP (1973), World Series MVP (1975), 17 All-Star Games, two Gold Gloves, one Silver Slugger

Pete Rose

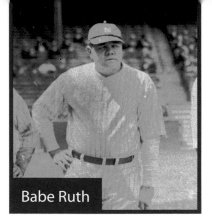

Babe Ruth

BABE RUTH OF-LHP

Boston Red Sox (1914–19), New York Yankees (1920–34), Boston Braves (1935)

Babe Ruth is perhaps the most famous baseball player of all time. He began his career as a pitcher, but his slugging talents eventually eclipsed his value on the mound. His 60 home runs in 1927 stood as MLB's single-season record until 1961, and his 714 career home runs were the most until Hank Aaron hit his 715th in 1974.

Games: 2,503	**AVG:** .342	**ERA:** 2.28
Hits: 2,873	**Innings Pitched:** 1,221.1	**Strikeouts:** 488
HRs: 714		
RBIs: 2,214	**W-L:** 94–46	
Awards: AL MVP (1923), two All-Star Games		

NOLAN RYAN RHP

New York Mets (1966, 1968–71), California Angels (1972–79), Houston Astros (1980–88), Texas Rangers (1989–93)

Nolan Ryan could throw a fastball at 100.9 miles per hour (162 kmh). He holds the MLB record for most career strikeouts and walks, and his seven no-hitters will be a hard record to top. On May 1, 1991, at age 44, he became the oldest pitcher to throw a no-hitter when he blanked the Toronto Blue Jays, striking out 16 batters in the process.

Games: 807
Innings Pitched: 5,386
W-L: 324–292
ERA: 3.19
Strikeouts: 5,714
Awards: Eight All-Star Games

MIKE SCHMIDT 3B

Philadelphia Phillies (1972–89)

A smooth third baseman with a steady glove and tremendous arm, Mike Schmidt would've been tough to get out of the lineup just based on his defense. But his powerful bat helped get him into the Hall of Fame. Schmidt led the NL in home runs eight times, including in 1980 when he hit a career-high 48 and won the first of his three NL MVP Awards. He also led the Phillies to their first title that year, hitting .381 with two homers and seven RBIs as Philadelphia knocked off the Kansas City Royals in six games.

Mike Schmidt

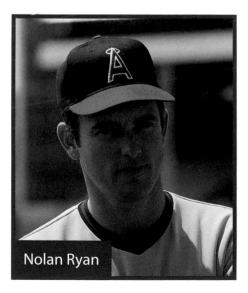
Nolan Ryan

Games: 2,404 **RBIs:** 1,595
Hits: 2,234   **AVG:** .267
HRs: 548
Awards: NL MVP (1980–81, 1986), World Series MVP (1980), 12 All-Star Games, ten Gold Gloves, six Silver Sluggers

TOM SEAVER RHP

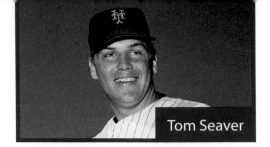

Tom Seaver

*New York Mets (1967–77, 1983),
Cincinnati Reds (1977–82),
Chicago White Sox (1984–86),
Boston Red Sox (1986)*

Games: 656
Innings Pitched: 4,783
W-L: 311–205
ERA: 2.86
Strikeouts: 3,640
Awards: NL Rookie of the Year (1967), NL Cy Young (1969, 1973, 1975), 12 All-Star Games

Tom Seaver was a huge part of the 1969 New York Mets, who won the World Series after seven years of mostly awful baseball. Seaver helped engineer that turnaround when he won 16 games in each of his first two seasons. Then he led the Mets to the title by going 25–7 with a 2.21 ERA. Seaver led the NL in strikeouts five times. He remains the Mets' career leader with 198 wins.

JOHN SMOLTZ RHP

*Atlanta Braves (1988–99,
2001–08), Boston Red Sox (2009),
St. Louis Cardinals (2009)*

Games: 723
Innings Pitched: 3,473
W-L: 213–155
Saves: 154
ERA: 3.33
Strikeouts: 3,084
Awards: NL Cy Young (1996), NLCS MVP (1992), eight All-Star Games, one Silver Slugger

John Smoltz was one of the best big-game pitchers in MLB history. His bulldog mentality on the mound helped lead the Atlanta Braves to five NL pennants and a World Series title in 1995. Smoltz posted a 15–4 record with a 2.67 ERA in the postseason. After suffering an arm injury, he reinvented himself as a closer. He's the only pitcher in MLB history with 200 victories and 150 saves.

John Smoltz

WARREN SPAHN LHP

Boston Braves (1942, 1946–52), Milwaukee Braves (1953–64), New York Mets (1965), San Francisco Giants (1965)

Warren Spahn holds the career record for most wins by a lefty and the most of any pitcher who played in the live-ball era. His unconventional high leg kick and effective screwball kept hitters off balance. Spahn led the NL in complete games nine times, including seven straight seasons beginning when he was 36 years old.

Warren Spahn

Games: 750
Innings Pitched: 5,243.2
W-L: 363–245
ERA: 3.09
Strikeouts: 2,583
Awards: Cy Young (1957), 17 All-Star Games

ICHIRO SUZUKI RF

Seattle Mariners (2001–12, 2018–19), New York Yankees (2012–14), Miami Marlins (2015–17)

Ichiro Suzuki took the league by storm when he came over from Japan in 2001 as a 27-year-old rookie. He was a speedy contact hitter with a strong arm. He slapped baseballs all over the park and won the MVP and Rookie of the Year awards that season. He remained one of the league's elite players for a decade. He notched his 3,000th MLB hit in 2016, at age 42. Add in his 1,278 hits from nine seasons in Japan and Ichiro has a claim to the title of Baseball's Hit King.

Ichiro Suzuki

Games: 2,653 **RBIs:** 780
Hits: 3,089   **AVG:** .311
HRs: 117
Awards: AL Rookie of the Year (2001), AL MVP (2001), ten All-Star Games, ten Gold Gloves, three Silver Sluggers

MIKE TROUT CF

Los Angeles Angels (2011–)

Mike Trout has put up MVP-caliber numbers throughout his days in Los Angeles. His career OPS of 1.0019 through 2021 was the highest of any active player and good for 11th all time. He also is known for home run-saving catches and a strong throwing arm in center field.

Games: 1,288 **RBIs:** 816
Hits: 1,419   **AVG:** .305
HRs: 310
Awards: AL Rookie of the Year (2012), AL MVP (2014, 2016, 2019), nine All-Star Games, eight Silver Sluggers

HONUS WAGNER SS

Louisville Colonels (1897–99), Pittsburgh Pirates (1900–17)

Honus Wagner was one of the game's greatest hitters. His eight NL batting titles were matched only by Tony Gwynn. Wagner also led the league in slugging six times and in stolen bases five times, making him a true triple-threat as a hitter. Playing in the dead-ball era, Wagner drove in at least 100 runs in nine seasons. He retired with the second-most hits in MLB history, and he's eighth on the all-time list.

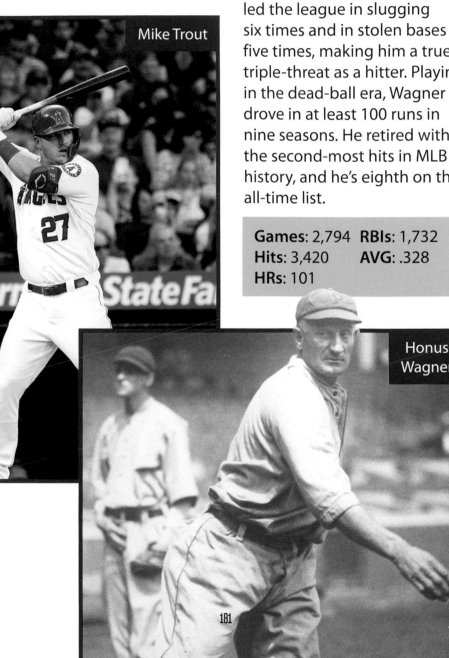

Mike Trout

Honus Wagner

Games: 2,794 **RBIs:** 1,732
Hits: 3,420 **AVG:** .328
HRs: 101

Ted Williams

TED WILLIAMS LF

Boston Red Sox (1939–42, 1946–60)

Ted Williams was one of the purest hitters the game has ever seen. His smooth left-handed swing produced six AL batting titles and four home run crowns. Williams was the last MLB player to hit .400 in a season, posting a .406 average in 1941. His career stats are even more amazing considering that he missed three full seasons and two partial seasons due to military service. Williams went out as a legend, hitting a home run at Fenway Park in his final career at bat.

Games: 2,292
Hits: 2,654
HRs: 521
RBIs: 1,839
AVG: .344
Awards: AL MVP (1946, 1949), 19 All-Star Games

Cy Young

CY YOUNG RHP

Cleveland Spiders (1890–98), St. Louis Perfectos (1899), St. Louis Cardinals (1900), Boston Americans (1901–07), Boston Red Sox (1908), Cleveland Naps (1909–11), Boston Rustlers (1911)

In 1956, MLB began giving an annual award to the best pitcher in the game. It's called the Cy Young Award, an honor befitting a man with his name plastered all over the baseball record books. The man with the most career wins, losses, games started (815), complete games (749), and innings pitched (7,356), Young thrived in the dead-ball era. He led the league in victories five times and threw three no-hitters, including one perfect game.

Games: 906
Innings Pitched: 7,356
W-L: 511–315
ERA: 2.63
Strikeouts: 2,803

HONORABLE MENTIONS

Pete Alexander (RHP): Philadelphia Phillies (1911–17, 1930), Chicago Cubs (1918–26), St. Louis Cardinals (1926–29)

Ernie Banks (SS-1B): Chicago Cubs (1953–71)

Cool Papa Bell (CF): Eight Negro League teams, including the Kansas City Monarchs (1932–34), Homestead Grays (1932, 1943–46), and Pittsburgh Crawfords (1933–38)

Bert Blyleven (RHP): Minnesota Twins (1970–76, 1985–88), Texas Rangers (1976–77), Pittsburgh Pirates (1978–80), Cleveland Indians (1981–85), California Angels (1989–90, 1992)

Wade Boggs (3B): Boston Red Sox (1982–92), New York Yankees (1993–97), Tampa Bay Devil Rays (1998–99)

George Brett (3B-1B): Kansas City Royals (1973–93)

Lou Brock (OF): Chicago Cubs (1961–64), St. Louis Cardinals (1964–79)

Miguel Cabrera (1B-3B-RF): Florida Marlins (2003–07), Detroit Tigers (2008–)

Eddie Collins (2B): Philadelphia Athletics (1906–14, 1927–30), Chicago White Sox (1915–26)

Martín Dihigo (RHP-2B): Four Negro Leagues teams, including the Cuban Stars (1923–27, 1930) and the Homestead Grays (1927–28)

Joe DiMaggio (CF): New York Yankees (1936–42, 1946–51)

Don Drysdale (RHP): Brooklyn Dodgers (1956–57), Los Angeles Dodgers (1958–69)

Rollie Fingers (RHP): Oakland Athletics (1968–76), San Diego Padres (1977–80), Milwaukee Brewers (1981–82, 1984–85)

Carlton Fisk (C): Boston Red Sox (1969, 1971–80), Chicago White Sox (1981–93)

Charlie Gehringer (2B): Detroit Tigers (1924–42)

Tom Glavine (LHP): Atlanta Braves (1987–2002, 2008), New York Mets (2003–07)

Hank Greenberg (1B-LF): Detroit Tigers (1930, 1933–41, 1945–46), Pittsburgh Pirates (1947)

Lefty Grove (LHP): Philadelphia Athletics (1925–33), Boston Red Sox (1934–41)

Roy Halladay (RHP): Toronto Blue Jays (1998–2009), Philadelphia Phillies (2010–13)

Trevor Hoffman (RHP): Florida Marlins (1993), San Diego Padres (1993–2008), Milwaukee Brewers (2009–10)

Carl Hubbell (LHP): New York Giants (1928–43)

Catfish Hunter (RHP): Kansas City Athletics (1965–67), Oakland Athletics (1968–74), New York Yankees (1975–79)

Reggie Jackson (RF): Kansas City Athletics (1967), Oakland Athletics (1968–75, 1987), Baltimore Orioles (1976), New York Yankees (1977–81), California Angels (1982–86)

Shoeless Joe Jackson (OF): Philadelphia Athletics (1908–09), Cleveland Naps (1910–14), Cleveland Indians (1915), Chicago White Sox (1915–20)

Ferguson Jenkins (RHP): Philadelphia Phillies (1965–66), Chicago Cubs (1966–73, 1982–83), Texas Rangers (1974–75, 1978–81), Boston Red Sox (1976–77)

Chipper Jones (3B-LF): Atlanta Braves (1993, 1995–2012)

Al Kaline (RF): Detroit Tigers (1953–74)

Harmon Killebrew (1B, 3B, OF): Washington Senators (1954–60), Minnesota Twins (1961–74), Kansas City Royals (1975)

Chuck Klein (RF): Philadelphia Phillies (1928–33, 1936–39, 1940–44), Chicago Cubs (1934–36), Pittsburgh Pirates (1939)

Buck Leonard (1B): Negro Leagues: Homestead Grays (1934–50)

Christy Mathewson (RHP): New York Giants (1900–16), Cincinnati Reds (1916)

Willie McCovey (1B-LF): San Francisco Giants (1959–73, 1977–80), San Diego Padres (1974–76), Oakland Athletics (1976)

Paul Molitor (3B-2B-DH): Milwaukee Brewers (1978–92), Toronto Blue Jays (1993–95), Minnesota Twins (1996–98)

Eddie Murray (1B): Baltimore Orioles (1977–88, 1996), Los Angeles Dodgers (1989–91, 1997), New York Mets (1992–93), Cleveland Indians (1994–96), Anaheim Angels (1997)

Phil Niekro (RHP): Milwaukee Braves (1964–65), Atlanta Braves (1966–83, 1987), New York Yankees (1984–85), Cleveland Indians (1986–87), Toronto Blue Jays (1987)

Shohei Ohtani (DH-RHP): Los Angeles Angels (2018–)

David Ortiz (1B-DH): Minnesota Twins (1997–2002), Boston Red Sox (2003–16)

Mel Ott (RF): New York Giants (1926–47)

Gaylord Perry (RHP): San Francisco Giants (1962–71), Cleveland Indians (1972–75), Texas Rangers (1975–77, 1980), San Diego Padres (1978–79), New York Yankees (1980), Atlanta Braves (1981), Seattle Mariners (1982–83), Kansas City Royals (1983)

Mike Piazza (C-1B): Los Angeles Dodgers (1992–98), Florida Marlins (1998), New York Mets (1998–2005), San Diego Padres (2006), Oakland Athletics (2007)

Robin Roberts (RHP): Philadelphia Phillies (1948–61), Baltimore Orioles (1962–65), Houston Astros (1965–66), Chicago Cubs (1966)

Alex Rodriguez (SS-3B): Seattle Mariners (1994–2000), Texas Rangers (2001–03), New York Yankees (2004–13, 2015–16)

Max Scherzer (RHP): Arizona Diamondbacks (2008–09), Detroit Tigers (2010–14), Washington Nationals (2015–21), Los Angeles Dodgers (2021–)

Duke Snider (CF): Brooklyn Dodgers (1947–57), Los Angeles Dodgers (1958–62), New York Mets (1963), San Francisco Giants (1964)

Willie Stargell (LF-1B): Pittsburgh Pirates (1962–82)

Bruce Sutter (RHP): Chicago Cubs (1976–80), St. Louis Cardinals (1981–84), Atlanta Braves (1985–86, 1988)

Justin Verlander (RHP): Detroit Tigers (2005–17), Houston Astros (2017–20)

Smokey Joe Williams (RHP): Eleven Negro Leagues teams, including the New York Lincoln Giants (1911–23) and the Homestead Grays (1925–32)

Dave Winfield (OF): San Diego Padres (1973–80), New York Yankees (1981–88, 1990), California Angels (1990–91), Toronto Blue Jays (1992), Minnesota Twins (1993–94), Cleveland Indians (1995)

Carl Yastrzemski (LF-1B): Boston Red Sox (1961–83)

Robin Yount (SS-CF): Milwaukee Brewers (1974–93)

Dodger Stadium

HITTERS

GAMES PLAYED
1. Pete Rose _____ 3,562
2. Carl Yastrzemski _____ 3,308
3. Hank Aaron _____ 3,298
4. Rickey Henderson _____ 3,081
5. Ty Cobb _____ 3,034

AT BATS
1. Pete Rose _____ 14,053
2. Hank Aaron _____ 12,364
3. Carl Yastrzemski _____ 11,988
4. Cal Ripken Jr. _____ 11,551
5. Ty Cobb _____ 11,440

HITS
1. Pete Rose _____ 4,256
2. Ty Cobb _____ 4,189
3. Hank Aaron _____ 3,771
4. Stan Musial _____ 3,630
5. Tris Speaker _____ 3,514

DOUBLES
1. Tris Speaker _____ 792
2. Pete Rose _____ 746
3. Stan Musial _____ 725
4. Ty Cobb _____ 724
5. Albert Pujols* _____ 672

TRIPLES
1. Sam Crawford _____ 309
2. Ty Cobb _____ 295
3. Honus Wagner _____ 252
4. Jake Beckley _____ 244
5. Roger Connor _____ 233

HOME RUNS
1. Barry Bonds _____ 762
2. Hank Aaron _____ 755
3. Babe Ruth _____ 714
4. Alex Rodriguez _____ 696
5. Albert Pujols* _____ 679

RUNS
1. Rickey Henderson _____ 2,295
2. Ty Cobb _____ 2,245
3. Barry Bonds _____ 2,227
4. Hank Aaron _____ 2,174
4. Babe Ruth _____ 2,174

RBIs
1. Hank Aaron _____ 2,297
2. Babe Ruth _____ 2,214
3. Albert Pujols* _____ 2,150
4. Alex Rodriguez _____ 2,086
5. Cap Anson _____ 2,075

STOLEN BASES
1. Rickey Henderson _____ 1,406
2. Lou Brock _____ 938
3. Billy Hamilton _____ 914
4. Ty Cobb _____ 897
5. Tim Raines _____ 808

BATTING AVERAGE
1. Ty Cobb _____ .366
2. Oscar Charleston _____ .364
3. Rogers Hornsby _____ .358
4. Joe Jackson _____ .355
5. Jud Wilson _____ .351

ON-BASE PERCENTAGE
1. Ted Williams _____ .482
2. Babe Ruth _____ .474
3. John McGraw _____ .466
4. Billy Hamilton _____ .455
5. Oscar Charleston _____ .449

OPS
1. Babe Ruth _____ 1.163
2. Ted Williams _____ 1.116
3. Lou Gehrig _____ 1.080
4. Oscar Charleston _____ 1.063
5. Barry Bonds _____ 1.051

PITCHERS

GAMES
1. Jesse Orosco _____ 1,252
2. Mike Stanton _____ 1,178
3. John Franco _____ 1,119
4. Mariano Rivera _____ 1,115
5. Dennis Eckersley _____ 1,071

WINS
1. Cy Young _____ 511
2. Walter Johnson _____ 417
3. Pete Alexander _____ 373
3. Christy Mathewson _____ 373
4. Pud Galvin _____ 365

STRIKEOUTS
1. Nolan Ryan _____ 5,714
2. Randy Johnson _____ 4,875
3. Roger Clemens _____ 4,672
4. Steve Carlton _____ 4,136
5. Bert Blyleven _____ 3,701

COMPLETE GAMES
1. Cy Young _____ 749
2. Pud Galvin _____ 646
3. Tim Keefe _____ 554
4. Kid Nichols _____ 532
5. Walter Johnson _____ 531

LOSSES
1. Cy Young _____ 315
2. Pud Galvin _____ 310
3. Nolan Ryan _____ 292
4. Walter Johnson _____ 279
5. Phil Niekro _____ 274

ERA
1. Ed Walsh _____ 1.82
2. Addie Joss _____ 1.89
3. Jim Devlin _____ 1.90
4. Jack Pfiester _____ 2.02
5. Joe Wood _____ 2.03

SHUTOUTS
1. Walter Johnson _____ 110
2. Pete Alexander _____ 90
3. Christy Mathewson _____ 79
4. Cy Young _____ 76
5. Eddie Plank _____ 69

SAVES
1. Mariano Rivera _____ 652
2. Trevor Hoffman _____ 601
3. Lee Smith _____ 478
4. Francisco Rodríguez _____ 437
5. John Franco _____ 424

WHIP
1. Addie Joss _____ 0.9678
2. Ed Walsh _____ 0.9996
3. Mariano Rivera _____ 1.0003
4. Clayton Kershaw* _____ 1.0042
5. Jacob deGrom* _____ 1.0114

INNINGS PITCHED
1. Cy Young _____ 7,356.0
2. Pud Galvin _____ 6,003.1
3. Walter Johnson _____ 5,914.1
4. Phil Niekro _____ 5,404.0
5. Nolan Ryan _____ 5,386.0

RBIs: Runs Batted In
OPS: On-Base Plus Slugging Percentage
ERA: Earned-Run Average

WHIP: Walks and Hits Per Innings Pitched
* Indicates player is active as of 2021

GLOSSARY

ace

The top starting pitcher on a team.

bribe

Money or favors given or promised in order to influence the judgment or conduct of a person in a position of trust.

closer

The relief pitcher on a team used to close out victories.

dynasty

An extended period of excellence or success for a team.

expansion team

A new team added to an existing league.

integration

Incorporating people belonging to different groups (such as races) into areas of society where they have been excluded.

pennant

An American League or National League championship.

perfect game

A pitching performance in which no batter reaches base.

rivalry

Heated competition between two parties over a long period.

strike

A workers' protest that involves refusing to work until requests are met.

walk-off

A victory that ends on the game's final at bat, causing the defense to walk off the field while the winning team celebrates.

FURTHER READINGS

Gitlin, Marty. *MLB*. Abdo, 2021.

Harris, Duchess, with Alex Kies. *The Negro Leagues*. Abdo, 2020.

Ventura, Marne. *STEM in Baseball*. Abdo, 2018.

ONLINE RESOURCES

To learn more about MLB, please visit **abdobooklinks.com** or scan this QR code. These links are routinely monitored and updated to provide the most current information available.

INDEX

PHOTO CREDITS

Cover Photos: Rich Pilling/Major League Baseball/Getty Images, front (Ken Griffey Jr.); Photo File/Hulton Archive/Getty Images, front (Jackie Robinson); Gregory Bull/AP Images, front (Fernando Tatis Jr.); Tony Tomsic/AP Images, front (Pete Rose); Elaine Thompson/AP Images, front (Mike Trout); Rob Tringali/Major League Baseball/Getty Images, front (Derek Jeter); Hy Peskins/Alon Alexander/Alamy, front (Willie Mays); Bettmann/Getty Images, back (Lefty Gomez); G Fiume/Getty Images Sport/Getty Images, back (Juan Soto)

Interior Photos: Ted S. Warren/AP Images, 1, 76; David Durochik/AP Images, 3, 46, 171 (top); AP Images, 4, 5, 6, 7, 8, 10–11, 12–13, 14, 15, 16–17, 18, 32, 37, 42, 44, 58, 66, 74, 80–81, 89, 97, 99, 102, 109, 114, 115, 119, 122, 124, 129, 148, 150, 151 (bottom), 153 (bottom), 154, 155 (bottom), 156 (top), 156 (bottom), 157, 158 (top), 158 (bottom), 161 (bottom), 164, 167 (top), 168 (top), 169, 170, 173 (bottom), 174, 176, 178, 179 (bottom), 182; Mark Duncan/AP Images, 19, 67; David J. Phillip/AP Images, 20–21, 47, 103, 111, 153 (top); Amy Sancetta/AP Images, 22–23, 51; Bill Kostroun/AP Images, 24–25, 180; John Bazemore/AP Images, 27, 31; Derrick Tuskan/AP Images, 28, 116–117; Matt York/AP Images, 29; Doug Mills/AP Images, 33; Wilfredo Lee/AP Images, 35, 84–85, 133; Ron Frehm/AP Images, 36, 52, 98; Chris O'Meara/AP Images, 38, 139; Bob Daugherty/AP Images, 39; Peter Southwick/ AP Images, 40; Christopher Katsarov/Canadian Press/AP Images, 41; Elise Amendola/AP Images, 43, 132; Aaron Doster/AP Images, 45; Charles Rex Arbogast/AP Images, 48, 108; Charles Krupa/AP Images, 49; Al Behrman/AP Images, 53; Harry Cabluck/AP Images, 55; Frank Jansky/Icon Sportswire/AP Images, 56; Gary Gardiner/AP Images, 59; David Zalubowski/AP Images, 60, 61; Jack Dempsey/AP Images, 63; Jim Mone/AP Images, 65; Getty Images Sport/Getty Images, 68; Focus on Sport/Getty Images, 69, 77, 110, 120, 175; Matt Slocum/AP Images, 70–71; Colin E. Braley/AP Images, 72–73; Orlin Wagner/AP Images, 75; Stephen Dunn/Allsport/Getty Images Sport/Getty Images, 79; Jeff Chiu/AP Images, 82, 106, 123, 128; Tony Gutierrez/AP Images, 83, 136; James A. Finley/AP Images, 86; Kathy Willens/AP Images, 87; Jeff Roberson/AP Images, 88; John Swart/AP Images, 90, 112; Steve Pyle/AP Images, 91; Otto Greule/Allsport/Getty Images Sport Classic/Getty Images, 92; Nick Wosika/Icon Sportswire/AP Images, 93; Ann Heisenfelt/AP Images, 95; Austin McAfee/Cal Sport Media/Zuma Wire/AP Images, 96–97; Mark Rucker/Transcendental Graphics/Getty Images Sport/Getty Images, 100, 181 (bottom); Adam Hunger/AP Images, 101; Ronald C. Modra/Getty Images Sport Classic/Getty Images, 104, 177 (bottom); Bob Galbraith/AP Images, 105; Lenny Ignelzi/AP Images, 107, 161 (top); Aaron Gash/AP Images, 113; Frank Polich/AP Images, 118; J. D./AP Images, 121; Jim Bryant/AP Images, 125; John Bunch/Icon Sportswire/AP Images, 127; Joe Puetz/AP Images, 131; Steve Nesius/AP Images, 134; Sue Ogrocki/AP Images, 135; Reed Saxon/AP Images, 137; Stubblebine/AP Images, 138; Rusty Kennedy/AP Images, 140, 155 (top), 179 (top); Eric Risberg/AP Images, 141; Marcio Jose Sanchez/AP Images, 142; Ed Reinke/AP Images, 143; Lawrence Jackson/AP Images, 144; Nick Wass/AP Images, 145, 163; Eric Gay/AP Images, 146–147; Tony Tomsic/AP Images, 149, 168 (bottom); Kristy MacDonald/AP Images, 151 (top); Tony Tomsic/Getty Images Sport Classic/Getty Images, 152; John Froschauer/AP Images, 159; Fred Jewell/AP Images, 160; Paul Sancya/AP Images, 162; Photo Works/Shutterstock Images, 165 (top); Robert Houston/AP Images, 165 (bottom); Brian Kersey/AP Images, 166; Mitchell Layton/Getty Images Sport/Getty Images, 167 (bottom); Bill Boyce/AP Images, 171 (bottom); Roberto Borea/AP Images, 172; Tammy Lechner/AP Images, 173 (top); Paul Shane/AP Images, 177 (top); Brian Rothmuller/Icon Sportswire/AP Images, 181 (top); George Grantham Bain Collection/Library of Congress, 183; Adam Kaz/iStockphoto, 186; iStockphoto, 187

Previously titled The MLB Encyclopedia for Kids

First Edition
First Printing, 2021

 THIS BOOK CONTAINS
RECYCLED MATERIALS

Editor: Alyssa Sorenson
Series Designer: Colleen McLaren
Cover Designer: Jake Slavik

ISBN: 978-1-952455-08-7 (paperback)

Library of Congress Control Number: 2021917063

Distributed in paperback by North Star Editions, Inc.
2297 Waters Drive
Mendota Heights, MN 55120
www.northstareditions.com

Printed in the United States of America